LIVE A PRAYING LIFE® WITHOUT FEAR

LET FAITH TAME YOUR WORRIES

JENNIFER KENNEDY DEAN

Other New Hope® books by Jennifer Kennedy Dean

Synced
Set Apart
Prayer Fatigue
Conversations with the Most High
Live a Praying Life®!
Live a Praying Life® in Adversity
Heart's Cry
Clothed with Power
Clothed with Power DVD
Power in the Blood of Christ
Power in the Name of Jesus
Altar'd
Pursuing the Christ
The Power of Small
Live a Praying Life® Bible Study—Tenth Anniversary Edition
Live a Praying Life® DVD Leader Kit—Tenth Anniversary Edition
Live a Praying Life® Journal
Life Unhindered!
Set Apart DVD Leader Kit
Secrets Jesus Shared
Secrets Jesus Shared DVD Leader Kit

"There are two ways to live—by fear or by faith. My friend, Jennifer Kennedy Dean, can move you from being wrapped up in fear to being enveloped in God's love, care, plan, and path. I have seen her overcome fears in her own life as she walked her path of faith. In *Live a Praying Life® Without Fear*, Jennifer shares her wealth of wisdom with you so you too can victoriously overcome fear!"

—*Pam Farrel, author of 45 books including* 7 Simple Skills for Every Woman: Success in Keeping Everything Together *and best-selling* Men Are Like Waffles, Women Are Like Spaghetti

"Not only is Jennifer Kennedy Dean one of the most excellent Bible teachers I have ever studied under, her words are absolutely clear and infinitely practical. Surrounded by a culture of fear, we often give in because of the people and situations we cannot control. Focusing on the deep questions that consume us, *Live a Praying Life® Without Fear* systematically opens up the Word of God to reveal how our prayers can actively fight fear through trust, faith, soul transformation, and embracing God's sovereignty. Interspersed with the rich insight, we learn from Jennifer's own experience of when everything she feared actually happened . . . and she survived. I highly recommend this study—but only for worriers and silent sufferers. In other words, everyone!"

—*Lucinda Secrest McDowell, author of* Dwelling Places *and founder of the Encouraging Words blog site*

"If you've ever wondered about God's sovereignty, read this book. If you've ever doubted God's sovereignty, read this book. If you're going through a difficult time and it seems like God's sovereignty isn't true, read this book. Your faith will grow and your trust in God's supreme power and control will chase away any doubt or distrust. Jennifer Kennedy Dean skillfully uses biblical insights about God's sovereignty to increase our faith and trust. She convinces us we have nothing to fear because God is in control and nothing can change the plan He knows is best."

—*Kathy Collard Miller, speaker and author of many books including* Never Ever Be the Same: A New You Starts Today

"If you are ready to conquer the fear that grips most of us, you can conquer it by prayer and faith. And nobody explains how as clearly, as deeply, as fully as does my friend Jennifer Kennedy Dean."

—*Gracie Malone, author of* Unafraid

"Once again, Jennifer Kennedy Dean challenges us anew to live a praying life. *Live a Praying Life® Without Fear* is a deep and unique look at fear, fear's effects on us, and the means available to us for dismantling this enemy. In four sections—the Purpose, Process, Promise, and Practice of Prayer—Jennifer is at her most compassionate and practical best. *Live a Praying Life® Without Fear* is perfect for personal and small group study, and the powerful applications promise rich growth and deep healing. As I journeyed through the book, prayer shifted from something I should do to something I long to do."

—*Jane Rubietta, international speaker and author of 19 books including* Worry Less So You Can Live More

"With a compelling yet warm writing style and a heart full of faith, Jennifer Kennedy Dean not only inspires readers but also provides a practical and biblical guide to breaking free from the bondage of fear. I highly recommend *Live a Praying Life® Without Fear!*"

—*Cheri Fuller, speaker and author of* Dangerous Prayer: Discovering Your Amazing Story Inside the Eternal Story of God

"When Jennifer Kennedy Dean challenges us to live without fear—to pray without fear—it's not just vague, spiritual-sounding advice. She gives us profound, faith-affirming teaching filled with powerful illustrations that will help us truly grasp the purpose, the process, the promise, and the practice of prayer. It's life-changing stuff!"

—*Christin Ditchfield, author of* What Women Should Know about Facing Fear: Finding Freedom from Anxious Thoughts, Nagging Worries, and Crippling Fears

LIVE A PRAYING LIFE® WITHOUT FEAR

LET FAITH TAME YOUR WORRIES

JENNIFER KENNEDY DEAN

NEW HOPE®
PUBLISHERS
Gospel-Centered. Missions-Driven.
BIRMINGHAM, ALABAMA

New Hope° Publishers
PO Box 12065
Birmingham, AL 35202-2065
NewHopePublishers.com
New Hope Publishers is a division of WMU°.

Library of Congress Cataloging-in-Publication Data
Names: Dean, Jennifer Kennedy, author.
Title: Live a praying life without fear : let faith tame your worries /
  Jennifer Kennedy Dean.
Description: Birmingham, AL : New Hope Publishers, 2016.
Identifiers: LCCN 2016030164 | ISBN 9781625915092 (sc)
Subjects: LCSH: Prayer—Christianity. | Fear—Religious
  aspects—Christianity. | Spiritual exercises.
Classification: LCC BV210.3 .D4355 2016 | DDC 248.3/2—dc23 LC record available at
https://lccn.loc.gov/2016030164

ISBN-13: 978-1-62591-509-2

N174108 • 1116 • 3M1

I sought the LORD, and he answered me; *heard* *and*

he delivered me from all my fears.

—PSALM 34:4

KJV

TABLE OF CONTENTS

PREFACE   11

INTRODUCTION   12

WEEK ONE
THE PURPOSE OF PRAYER   17

DAY ONE   The Anatomy of Fear   18
DAY TWO   The Sovereignty of God   32
DAY THREE   The Power of God   40
DAY FOUR   The Truth of God   52
DAY FIVE   The Presence of God   60

WEEK TWO
THE PROCESS OF PRAYER   67

DAY ONE   The Effect of Fear   68
DAY TWO   The Purveyor of Fear   74
DAY THREE   The Habit of Fear   80
DAY FOUR   The End of Fear   88
DAY FIVE   The Reframing of Fear   92

WEEK THREE
THE PROMISE OF PRAYER
103

DAY ONE	Recognizing the Truth	104
DAY TWO	Rewriting the Script	110
DAY THREE	Embracing the Weakness	118
DAY FOUR	Uncovering the Hidden Fears	128
DAY FIVE	Embracing the Presence	138

WEEK FOUR
THE PRACTICE OF PRAYER
145

DAY ONE	Take Action: Praise	146
DAY TWO	Take Action: Apply Truth	150
DAY THREE	Take Action: Reach Out	154
DAY FOUR	Take Action: Pray in New Ways	158
DAY FIVE	Take Action: Exchange Lies for Truth	162

CONCLUSION
167

PREFACE

FEAR IS ONE OF SATAN'S MOST POTENT WEAPONS AGAINST BELIEVERS. The brain—the seat of our thoughts, emotions, memories, and beliefs—is his theater of operation. I believe Scripture gives us the strategy for opposing and overcoming his assaults, robbing fear of its power.

The way God has created our brains has been a fascination of mine. I have written and taught on the topic for years. I have a huge library of research materials on the subject. I have studied and absorbed information on the brain and its functions because I am so engrossed by the idea that as we discover more about the physical organ we call the brain, it becomes clear that God has constructed our brains in such a way that He can transform our thinking, heal the pain of memories, and set us free.

I find that the more I understand some process, the more I am likely to cooperate with God's strategy. So, in this study, we'll take a look at how God's design of your brain works for His purposes in setting you free from fear.

While I am passionate about this topic, have done years of research on it, and am confident in the information herein, I've not conducted these scientific studies on the brain myself. This book is not intended to be a scientific resource. For our purposes, we are going to examine the function of the brain as it relates to our interaction with fear.

INTRODUCTION

FEAR IS YOUR ENEMY'S BEST WEAPON. He uses it skillfully and often to great effect. Fear and its offshoots—worry and anxiety—are like a wildfire, encroaching on every area of your life and leaving destruction in their wake. Fear eats its way into your emotions, robbing you of the peace and rest God intends for you. Fear burrows into your relationships and colors your interactions with those you love. Fear robs your body of its vigor, occupies your thoughts, and monopolizes your attention. Fear hijacks your life.

"Do not fear" is one of God's oft-repeated injunctions and encouragements. Because fear is so useful to your enemy, God works tirelessly to free you from its grip. Your Father wants you to live fully and experience all of the abundant life He paid so high a price for you to have. He works aggressively to lead you out of fear and into faith.

In this study, we will wrestle with the realities of a world that presents much fodder for fear. We will learn how to interrupt the cycle of fear and bring the realities of faith to bear. We will learn how to activate faith in the face of fear. We will discover practical solutions for how to live fueled by faith instead of fueled by fear.

In these weeks together, we will address these topics:

WHAT IS FEAR?

We fear when situations and people are not under our control. Fear is a feeling of powerlessness. We can't control outcomes, events, or people. Anything you can control does not cause fear.

12

HOW DOES FEAR GET A FOOTHOLD IN OUR LIVES?

As we recognize our vulnerabilities, we begin to fear. It comes naturally to us and puts down deep roots. Unless we guard against it, we grow in fear instead of growing in faith.

WHY DO WE FIND GOD SAYING TIME AND AGAIN, "DO NOT FEAR"?

Because there is much to fear. Fear is a natural first response. He is saying, "What you can't control is fully under My control."

HOW ELSE CAN WE LEARN NOT TO FEAR EXCEPT BY EXPERIENCING FEARFUL CIRCUMSTANCES?

If there were nothing to cause fear or anxiety, then there would be no need for Him to say, "Do not fear." We will all find ourselves in circumstances that have the potential to produce fear, and God will use those circumstances to make us fearless.

WHAT ABOUT WHEN THE THING YOU FEAR HAPPENS?

How do we process the fact that bad and scary things will indeed happen? Is there no magic formula to keep difficulty and heartache away? You will find that what you feared would break you will instead build you. We can learn how to frame our situations in the context of who God is, and that will recalibrate our response. That is what we are exploring throughout this study, so we will revisit this concept many times.

THE KEY

Living without fear is not believing that nothing fearful will happen but, rather, believing that nothing will happen apart from

God's intervening grace. Nothing will happen without the hand of God in control, filtering out what will destroy, softening the full force of the blow, and bringing a result that could not be accomplished any other way. His standard for weighing your situation in the balance before it reached you is: the glory it will produce outweighs the pain it will cause.

We will look to Scripture to teach us how to experience life differently—from a faith view rather than from a fear view. We'll learn how to navigate life differently so that fear does not commandeer our thoughts and take our emotions hostage. We will examine how our thoughts and emotions work, as designed by God, so that we learn to let God make full use of His amazing architecture—the way He has structured our minds and our emotions.

We will explore what God has to say about how to live a praying life without fear, using the principles of the *Live a Praying Life®* study: The Purpose of Prayer, The Process of Prayer, The Promise of Prayer, and The Practice of Prayer.

Join me. Let's tackle life's challenges together in the light of God's Word, made present and specific by His Holy Spirit. Let's ask His Holy Spirit to hand deliver the Father's truth to our hungry hearts.

Write out your prayer for this study by completing these statements:

I CONFESS

_____
_____
_____
_____

I DESIRE

_____
_____
_____
_____

I BELIEVE

_____
_____
_____
_____

I COMMIT

_____
_____
_____
_____

DATE:

_____

In Jesus' name,
SIGNED:

_____

THE PURPOSE OF PRAYER

The purpose of prayer is to release the power of God to accomplish the purposes of God. The purpose of prayer is to discover God's will, not obligate Him to do mine; to reflect God's mind, not change it.

Prayer is the means by which you will be freed from your earthbound, time bound thinking to participate in eternity. True prayer releases His power so that His power can accomplish immeasurably more than we can ask or even imagine (Ephesians 3:20).

—Live a Praying Life®

DAY ONE
THE ANATOMY OF FEAR

WHAT CAUSES FEAR? What awakens fear? Babies are born with few fears. The fear of falling appears to be an inborn fear. We are also born with a startle response to loud noises, but that is more likely a physiological response. Every other fear is learned. Why do some people fear certain things while others fear something altogether different? Why don't we all fear the same things to the same degree? If fear were logical, then it seems that we would all fear the same things equally.

Let's take some time to understand the anatomy of fear. As we begin, let's acknowledge that some fear is healthy and has the job of keeping us safe. That's not the kind of fear we are addressing. We are going to deal with the kind of fear and worry that has no beneficial effect and that keeps you bound instead of keeping you safe.

Take a minute and think about what you fear, what you worry about, or what causes you anxiety. I've listed some commonly fearful areas. (See p. 19.) You fill in the details about your particular fears in that area. Be specific. What do you fear will happen? You may have some anxieties that are not on this list, so add those. As you do this exercise, don't feel condemned or ashamed. Let the tender leading of the Spirit direct you to all truth. That's His job. "But when the Friend comes, the Spirit of the Truth, he will take you by the hand and guide you into all the truth there is" (John 16:13 *The Message*). Unless we pull things out into the light, they can wreak havoc in our lives. But, most often, whatever the Holy Spirit shines light on is where He intends to bring truth and healing.

> FOR GOD, WHO SAID, "LET LIGHT SHINE OUT OF DARKNESS," MADE HIS LIGHT SHINE IN OUR HEARTS TO GIVE US THE LIGHT OF THE KNOWLEDGE OF GOD'S GLORY DISPLAYED IN THE FACE OF CHRIST.
> —2 CORINTHIANS 4:6

This is just between you and Him. He loves you and is gentle with you. **Identify the fears you experience, and write out some detail about how that fear shows up in your life.**

CHILDREN

_____

MARRIAGE

_____

MONEY

_____

POSITION

_____

PEOPLE'S OPINIONS OF YOU

_____

BEING EMBARRASSED

_____

POSSESSIONS

_____

HEALTH

_____

INJURY

_____

DYING

_____

FAILURE

_____

RISK

_____

CHANGE

_____

OTHER

_____

Now, go back to the list and circle the fears that are pervasive enough that you recognize their effects on your life. They hold you back, cripple your relationships, or occupy too much of your thoughts and keep you from peace.

OUT OF CONTROL

In each case, I think you will find that what makes a particular fear fearful is that you cannot control its outcome and the outcome matters to you. Would you say that is true? If you can control an outcome, then there is nothing to fear, or if the outcome does not have significance to you, then the potential outcome does not engender fear.

Let's tackle the issue of control first. Can you acknowledge, for each of your fears, that you have no control over the outcome? In that sense, you are helpless. For many of us, our approach to prayer is in the hope that we can find the prayer key that will allow us to control the outcome and make things go as we think best. In the beginning of my journey to learn to live a praying life, here is what I discovered about my own motivations and the Lord seemed to ask me why I wanted to know how to pray:

> God peeled back the layers of my practiced, memorized, other people's answers until my truth emerged . . . "Father, I want to know how to pray so that I will know how to get You to do *what* I want You to do *when* I want You to do it. I hope to learn how to make the best possible use of prayer for my benefit."
> —*Live a Praying Life*®

Often, the content of our prayers is pleading with God to make the outcome conform to our expectations. We look for formulas and secrets that will make our prayers effective, by which we mean prayers that will get God to carry out our best ideas. Anxiety mounts because the effect of our prayers, we believe, is in some way dependent on whether we have said it right, had enough faith, lived righteously enough, or whatever we have come to believe will give our prayers the necessary boost.

Look at the fallacies here. First, that you think you know what God should do. Second, that God is waiting for you to convince Him to do good for you and your loved ones. Third, that prayer's effect is dependent on you.

FALLACY #1:
YOU KNOW WHAT GOD SHOULD DO

God is full of surprises. How He will work in any given circumstance is not governed by your best ideas. He loves you too much to limit Himself to your thoughts and ways. He is not waiting for you to give Him the answer, He is inviting you to give Him the need. You don't have to bring Him the answer. Just hand over the need. Let Him meet your need in His way and in His time. He wants you to learn to be open to His ways, which are higher than your ways, and His ideas, which are far beyond any you could possibly come up with.

> IF GOD WERE LIMITED TO THE FARTHEST REACHES OF YOUR IMAGINATION, THEN HE WOULD DELIVER LESS THAN HIS BEST.

If God were limited to the farthest reaches of your imagination, then He would deliver less than His best. He knows what you do not, so His plan is based on full knowledge and understanding.

You can trust God's plans and intentions. His every thought toward you and those you love is only, always good. He is not working on your timetable or according to your prescribed solution. But He is working for your good and for the good of those you love. He is ingenious in His ways, working in the smallest details, on the micro level, and also on the macro level—working out events and situations that will impact and change the course of situations years, even generations, down the road.

> God's work in our lives in response to prayer is an ongoing eternal design instead of many isolated plans. God's will flows through circumstances. His work in one circumstance sets the stage for the next. Over the course of time, there will be circumstances that, although you have prayed, seem not to have worked out according to God's revealed will. But wait! Watch to see what God does next. Watch to see which element

of your disappointing circumstance is the catalyst for the next victory. Watch how the immediate flows into the ultimate.

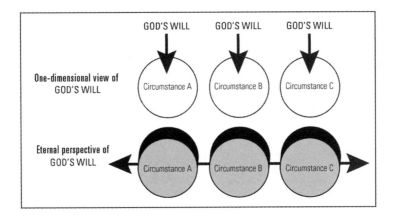

Don't focus your faith on a specific outcome; focus your faith on God. —*Live a Praying Life*®

We are very focused on relief right now. This minute. God has His eye on the whole unfolding plan. He knows how to resolve the current circumstance that is causing you to fear in such a way that it lays the groundwork for the next thing that will come into play, which will prepare the ground for the next piece of the plan, until you see how one thing flowed to the next and realize that God has been working out a result that was impossible without each circumstance.

God is not haphazard, but strategic. He does not allow anything to come into your life that is not compatible with and necessary to His plan for your good, your ultimate happiness, your benefit. You can trust that when prayer releases the power of God for the purposes of God into your circumstances, you will see His goodness. This is why your heart can rest in Him. When you turn to Him in faith and surrender, He will respond with all His power and all His provision.

––––––––––

In each of your specific fears (take them one by one), can you acknowledge that God knows what you do not? Look up each Scripture, and then write out your personal agreement with its truth. Spend time surrendering each fear to the truth of His Word.

PROVERBS 27:1

JOB 11:7–9

ISAIAH 55:9 and PSALM 103:11 *(Read these together. His ways are higher, but His love is also higher.)*

ROMANS 11:33–36

ISAIAH 40:13

In each of your specific fears (take them one by one), can you acknowledge that God's intentions and plans are only good, loving, and beneficial?

PROVERBS 23:18

 ISAIAH 30:18

✳ ISAIAH 40:31

whole chapter

✳ PSALM 31:19

✳ ROMANS 8:32

FALLACY #2:
GOD IS WAITING FOR YOU TO CONVINCE HIM

God intends your good. He does not need to be persuaded to love you, plan for you, or work on your behalf. On the contrary. He is eager for you to receive all He has to offer. "Do not be afraid, little flock, for your Father has been pleased to give you the kingdom" (Luke 12:32). Everything He has available for you in His kingdom, He is _pleased_—has chosen gladly, takes pleasure in, delights in—_pleased_ to give you.

He sees your dilemma—whether it is something real occurring in your life or something you are afraid might happen in the future. He sees it, and He knows all about it. He knows the basis of that fear. He sees and knows, and He has a plan for how to relieve you of your fear.

He knew about your situation before you did and planned in advance to deliver you. "Before they call I will answer; while they are still speaking I will hear" (Isaiah 65:24). Your salvation was accomplished before the world began (Revelation 13:8). Before the problem arose, the answer was ready.

"The inhabitants of the earth whose names have not been written in the book of life from the creation of the world" (Revelation 17:8). Compare to Luke 10:20 and Philippians 4:3. **When were names written in the Book of Life?**

"For he chose us in him before the creation of the world to be holy and blameless in his sight" (Ephesians 1:4). **When did God know you and set you apart to be His?**

"He has saved us and called us to a holy life—not because of anything we have done but because of his own purpose and grace. This grace was given us in Christ Jesus before the beginning of time" (2 Timothy 1:9). **When was grace given to you in Christ Jesus?**

"Then the King will say to those on his right, 'Come, you who are blessed by my Father; take your inheritance, the kingdom prepared for you since the creation of the world'" (Matthew 25:34). **When was the kingdom prepared for believers?**

"Paul, a servant of God and an apostle of Jesus Christ to further the faith of God's elect and their knowledge of the truth that leads to godliness—in the hope of eternal life, which God, who does not lie, promised before the beginning of time, and which now at his appointed season he has brought to light through the preaching entrusted to me by the command of God our Savior" (Titus 1:1–3). **When was eternal life promised? When was eternal life readied and prepared? When was that which was prepared before time brought to light—manifested, revealed?**

———————————————————————————————————

———————————————————————————————————

"For we are God's handiwork, created in Christ Jesus to do good works, which God prepared in advance for us to do" (Ephesians 2:10). **When were the works assigned to you prepared?**

———————————————————————————————————

———————————————————————————————————

Do you see God's pattern? He loves you so much—is so eager to provide for you—that He figured it all out in advance. You don't have to convince Him to provide for you. You only need to embrace what He has made available to your life.

FALLACY #3: PRAYER'S EFFICACY DEPENDS ON YOU

God designed prayer, and He designed it to work. He instituted prayer as the conduit through which the power of heaven flows into the circumstances of earth. Prayer is a force that reaches into the heavenly realms, grabs hold of the power and provision of God, and pulls it into the circumstances of earth. God has not set us up for failure. He has not devised a method that would be tricky and difficult so that it only works under highly controlled conditions.

Prayer works because God is faithful and responds to the prayers of His people, even when those prayers are imperfect and indefinite. Even when those prayers are offered by ragged, tattered, flawed believers. His response to prayer is not in doing as we demand, but in releasing His power, His provision, and His intervening will as a response to the prayers of His people. He responds to our heart's cry, even when our words miss the mark.

Many people consider their prayers to be answered when God does what they have told Him to do and unanswered when God does not work in the way they have instructed Him. This leads to the idea that prayer often does not work, and so we need to work harder, try harder, to find some way to improve our prayer performance so that we will have better results.

People often struggle with the question, "What if my situation that is causing me to fear is of my own making?" Honestly, many of our situations are, to some extent, of our own making. Does God tell us, "You made your bed, now you'll have to lie in it. Get yourself out of this on your own"? Of course not! Consider what Charles H. Spurgeon had to say on the matter in his book, *The Treasury of David*:

> We may seek God even when we have sinned. If sin could blockade the mercy-seat it would be all over with us, but the mercy is that there are gifts even for the rebellious, and an advocate for men who sin.

Oswald Chambers states in his classic book, *My Utmost for His Highest*:

> "I will never leave you . . ."—not for any reason; not my sin, selfishness, stubbornness, nor waywardness. Have I really let God say to me that He will never leave me? If I have not truly heard this assurance of God, then let me listen again.

Does sin matter? Yes. Sin diminishes my ability to perceive God's voice and His guidance. Do I have to be sinless and perfect for my prayers to have effect? No. If that were true, no prayer would ever be answered.

Does faith matter? Yes. But not as a commodity that you come up with and then trade in for favors. Rather, faith is given as a gift from God and grows as you learn to operate your life in faith. The more you live by faith and not by sight, the more you see and understand how God is working in response to prayer.

> TO GROW IN PRAYER AND DEVELOP A DEEPER WALK WITH THE FATHER, YOU WON'T NEED TO SEARCH FOR A BETTER METHOD OR FORMULA, YOU SIMPLY NEED TO ALIGN YOUR LIFE AND YOUR HEART WITH HIM.

To grow in prayer and develop a deeper walk with the Father, you won't need to search for a better method or formula, you simply need to align your life and your heart with Him. Pursue Him, not His gifts. His gifts are already yours for the taking.

> My goal is God Himself, not joy nor peace;
> Nor even blessing, but Himself, my God.
> 'Tis His to lead me there, not mine but His . . .
> At any cost, dear Lord, by any road.
> —*"My Goal,"* Frederick Brook

Do you recognize ways that you have been trying to find better methods for prayer in an effort to get God to act as you think He should?

_____

_____

Has this effort robbed you of peace in prayer?

_____

_____

_____

_____

DAY TWO
THE SOVEREIGNTY OF GOD

To live life as God intends—fearlessly—we have to be fully confident that God is completely in control. Otherwise, how can we let go of our need to manage and struggle to make things line up as we think they should? That is the very thing that keeps us in fear mode—worry and anxiety leeching the joy and peace from our lives. If we feel responsible for fixing and correcting circumstances and people, then we will never know peace. We weren't built to carry that load. We break down under the strain of it. Physically, emotionally, spiritually. It breaks us. And it makes no sense at all. Worry is not reasonable or realistic.

> Today, I exchange every worrying thought for thanksgiving. If the situations that worry me were indeed my responsibility—if You were looking to me to solve the problems and unravel the messes—then worry would make perfect sense. I'm not up to the job. I haven't a clue about how to resolve things. You are not depending on me for the answers. I'm looking to You for the answers. Thanksgiving and praise make more sense than worry. I acknowledge that all my stressing and worrying does not change anything except my state of mind. When I could be delighting in You and Your care, instead worry loads me down and steals all my joy. Today, I choose joy. —*Conversations With the Most High*, Jennifer Kennedy Dean

So, if prayer is the force that reaches into the heavenly realms and takes hold of the power and provision and plans of God, then unless God is fully in control of all things, we can't rest in that reality. What if there are gaps in God's sovereign control? Don't people have free will? Can't people make choices outside God's plan and bring disaster? Unless you settle these questions, fear will always have a foothold in your life. How can God tell us over and over that we need not fear—ever, under any circumstance—if He is not completely powerful and fully sovereign—always, under every circumstance?

SETTING THE RECORD STRAIGHT

As we progress in our understanding of prayer, we return again and again to the centerpiece, the cornerstone and foundational truth upon which every prayer principle rests: the sovereignty of God. This is the nucleus around which all truth orbits. This is the gravitational force that holds all the pieces together. God is sovereign.

The power of prayer lies in this: *it releases the power of God to accomplish the purposes of God.* This brings the thinking person to an apparent dilemma. If prayer always releases all the power of God, opening the way for Him to accomplish all of His purposes in His way and in His time, then how do we understand the free will of human beings as it pertains to prayer? In spite of prayer, couldn't a human choose not to cooperate with God and so frustrate the will of God in any given circumstance?

It's important to understand this because in nearly all cases, a human being's choices and actions are involved in the answer. If we believe that a human being can thwart or resist God's plan, then prayer will seem futile, and it will be impossible to pray with complete confidence. Fear and anxiety will maintain a choke hold on our lives.

The answer to every question is in the Word of God. It does no good to speculate or postulate. If we can come to the Word having laid aside all of our preconceived ideas and expectations and instead let the living, active Word of God speak, we will find answers that are both intellectually and spiritually satisfying.

God makes this promise to those who seek out truth from Him:

> MY SON, IF YOU WILL RECEIVE MY WORDS AND TREASURE MY COMMAND-MENTS WITHIN YOU, MAKE YOUR EAR ATTENTIVE TO WISDOM, INCLINE YOUR HEART TO UNDERSTANDING; FOR IF YOU CRY FOR DISCERNMENT, LIFT YOUR VOICE FOR UNDERSTANDING; IF YOU SEEK HER AS SILVER AND SEARCH FOR HER AS FOR HIDDEN TREASURES; THEN YOU WILL DISCERN THE FEAR OF THE LORD AND DISCOVER THE KNOWLEDGE OF GOD. FOR THE LORD GIVES WISDOM; FROM HIS MOUTH COME KNOWLEDGE AND UNDERSTANDING.
> —PROVERBS 2:1–6 NASB

From years of crying out for discernment and lifting my voice for understanding on this topic, I have reached some conclusions that I fully believe to be consistent with the whole counsel of God. I humbly present them to you in the pages that follow, asking that the precious Spirit would take all that is of Jesus and make it known to us (John 16:14–15).

Let me state clearly what we are addressing in this book. *How does the sovereignty of God operate when the will of a human being is involved in the answer to prayer?*

In the following Scriptures, underline or mark the words or phrases that describe God's sovereignty.

HIS DOMINION IS AN ETERNAL DOMINION; HIS KINGDOM ENDURES FROM GENERATION TO GENERATION. ALL THE PEOPLES OF THE EARTH ARE REGARDED AS NOTHING. HE DOES AS HE PLEASES WITH THE POWERS OF HEAVEN AND THE PEOPLES OF THE EARTH. NO ONE CAN HOLD BACK HIS HAND OR SAY TO HIM: "WHAT HAVE YOU DONE?" —DANIEL 4:34–35

FOR HE SPOKE, AND IT CAME TO BE; HE COMMANDED, AND IT STOOD FIRM. THE LORD FOILS THE PLANS OF THE NATIONS; HE THWARTS THE PURPOSES OF THE PEOPLES. BUT THE PLANS OF THE LORD STAND FIRM FOREVER, THE PURPOSES OF HIS HEART THROUGH ALL GENERATIONS. —PSALM 33:9–11

I MAKE KNOWN THE END FROM THE BEGINNING, FROM ANCIENT TIMES, WHAT IS STILL TO COME. I SAY, "MY PURPOSE WILL STAND, AND I WILL DO ALL THAT I PLEASE." —ISAIAH 46:10

JESUS ANSWERED, "YOU WOULD HAVE NO POWER OVER ME IF IT WERE NOT GIVEN TO YOU FROM ABOVE." —JOHN 19:11

THE FATHER LOVES THE SON AND HAS PLACED EVERYTHING IN HIS HANDS. —JOHN 3:35

No matter what is causing you fear or anxiety right now, God is sovereign. He knows what He is doing. You are not at the mercy of any person or circumstance. No detail of the circumstance or situation you fear is outside His jurisdiction.

Write out a proclamation of faith that contradicts the lies of your enemy who wants to replace faith with fear.

_____

_____

What lie is the enemy trying to convince you is true about God's sovereignty? Be as specific as you can.

_____

_____

_____

_____

What truth contradicts that very lie? Start with the words "I believe . . ."

_____

_____

_____

_____

WHAT ABOUT AN UNBELIEVING PERSON?

What if an unbelieving person or even a believer who is not pursuing God's ways is key to the circumstance creating fear in you—either fear of what might happen or fear and worry in the midst of trying circumstances?

Let's start by looking at how Scripture describes a lost person. What is the condition of a lost person?

_____

In each passage, mark the word or phrase that describes a person who is not a Christ follower.

AND EVEN IF OUR GOSPEL IS VEILED, IT IS VEILED TO THOSE WHO ARE PERISHING, IN WHOSE CASE THE (GOD) OF THIS WORLD HAS BLINDED THE MINDS OF THE UNBELIEVING SO THAT THEY MIGHT NOT SEE THE LIGHT OF THE GOSPEL OF THE GLORY OF CHRIST, WHO IS THE IMAGE OF GOD.
—2 CORINTHIANS 4:3–4 NASB

AND YOU WERE DEAD IN YOUR TRESPASSES AND SINS, IN WHICH YOU FORMERLY WALKED ACCORDING TO THE COURSE OF THIS WORLD, ACCORD-ING TO THE PRINCE OF THE POWER OF THE AIR, OF THE SPIRIT THAT IS NOW WORKING IN THE SONS OF DISOBEDIENCE. —EPHESIANS 2:1–2 NASB

WHEN YOU WERE DEAD IN YOUR TRANSGRESSIONS AND THE UNCIR-CUMCISION OF YOUR FLESH, HE MADE YOU ALIVE TOGETHER WITH HIM.
—COLOSSIANS 2:13 NASB

AND THAT THEY WILL COME TO THEIR SENSES AND ESCAPE FROM THE TRAP OF THE DEVIL, WHO HAS TAKEN THEM CAPTIVE TO DO HIS WILL.
—2 TIMOTHY 2:26

Let's consider each description the Scripture applies to those out-side Christ.

BLIND

One thing Scripture tells us about an unsaved person is that he or she is blind—*cannot* see. He is blinded by "the god of this world." There is an active and intentional strategy in play that blinds the mind of the unbeliever. The unbeliever, apart from the Holy Spirit, lacks the ability to see and understand the truth.

SPIRITUALLY DEAD

An unsaved person is spiritually dead. This person cannot

respond righteously to anything in the spiritual realm; he cannot comprehend spiritual truth. "But a natural man does not accept the things of the Spirit of God, for they are foolishness to him; and he cannot understand them, because they are spiritually appraised" (1 Corinthians 2:14 NASB).

To further complicate matters, the prince of the power of the air is "now working" in the unbeliever to keep him or her in the state of death. The word translated "at work" or "working" in Ephesians 2:2 is the Greek word *energeō*. It means to work fervently, with energy, and to be effective and powerful. It is the same word used of God's work in the believer. The enemy's forces are actively and efficiently operating in the unbeliever to keep him or her from the truth.

SLAVES

In John 8:31–47, Jesus makes clear that unbelievers are slaves. He does not bother to say so diplomatically. He says it clearly and without equivocation. The unbelievers who were debating Him at that moment give us meaningful insight into the mind of an unbeliever. They are outraged and offended that Jesus said they are not free. They insist that they are free. Jesus insists that they are not free. He says that, unwittingly, they are doing the will of the devil. Believing themselves to be free, they are carrying out Satan's agenda. Stop and read this passage. I want you to see how open this is. There is no couched language, no subtext. According to Jesus, freedom can come only one way: "If the Son makes you free, then you will be free indeed" (v. 36). Unbelievers are captives, but are deluded as to their condition. "The whole world lies in *the power of* the evil one" (1 John 5:19 NASB).

TO SUMMARIZE

The circumstance or potential occurrence that is causing you fear and worry might depend on a decision-maker who is not a Christ follower. That person has no interest in seeking God's direction. Yet, he or she is positioned to make decisions that will impact your life.

The reality that we have just examined about the condition of a lost person might seem discouraging to you right now. But wait until tomorrow's lesson. We will put the next piece into the puzzle, and you will see that no one calls the shots about your life except God. That lost person or the person who is not listening to the Father seems to have some control over your situation or your imagined situation, and that person is carrying out the plans of the enemy who seeks only to kill, steal, and destroy. Bad news. Or is it?

DAY THREE
THE POWER OF GOD

FOLLOWING UP ON YESTERDAY'S THOUGHTS, LET'S TAKE THE NEXT STEP. To review, a person who is not a Christ follower is in some way positioned to make decisions that will impact the situation you fear. Scripture shows us that the lost person is unwittingly following Satan's agenda and has no sensitivity to God's agenda. The matter about which you are praying will require an unbeliever to be influenced by God to do His will. Since this person has no relationship with God, how can we believe that through prayer his or her mind will be responsive to God's power?

That sounds discouraging until you realize that Satan's freedom is limited by God's sovereignty. Satan is only free to act if his actions will set the stage for God's purpose to be accomplished.

GOD'S PAWN

We have already established that the unbeliever is not acting freely but is acting in response to the spirit of rebellion now at work in him or her. But *Satan's freedom to operate is limited by God's sovereignty.* Satan's plans and schemes only come to fruition if they will set the stage for God's purpose to be accomplished. First, let's clearly establish this fact from Scripture.

Consider the dialogue between God and Satan in reference to Job (Job 1:6–12). How did Satan know that God had placed a protective hedge around Job and all his possessions (v. 10)? He knew because of the countless times he had tried to penetrate it. Until God gave permission, Satan was helpless and unable to breach

God's hedge. God only allowed Satan to touch Job under the strict-est guidelines. Why did God call Job to Satan's attention? Why did God goad Satan into targeting Job? I believe that Satan had given up on Job. I believe that Satan considered Job a lost cause. God opened the way for Satan to reach into Job's life

> BUT SATAN'S FREEDOM TO OPERATE IS LIMITED BY GOD'S SOVEREIGNTY.

because God wanted to accomplish something in Job that would require adversity in order for Job to come to the deepest possible understanding of who God is. At the end of his ordeal, Job has a breakthrough vision of God is his life: "My ears had heard of you but now my eyes have seen you" (Job 42:5).

Through this process Job became more, not less. Satan was God's tool. Until God was ready to make use of Satan's plans (in a limited form), Satan could not touch Job. When Satan touched Job, it set the stage for God's purpose.

God knows the thoughts of all people, even those who are hostile to Him. "[Jesus] did not need any testimony about mankind, for he knew all people" (John 2:25). He is able to use even the thoughts and plans in the heart of a person—both believers and unbelievers—to bring about His divine purposes.

Have you ever thought about how detailed and exactly timed the arrest, trial, Crucifixion, burial, and Resurrection of Jesus was? The exact timing had been established before the world began. God gave an elaborate and explicit picture of the timing when He established the feasts in the Old Covenant, generations before the event occurred in history. Let's take a look at some of the details of God's perfect timing in the life and death of Christ. (For a more detailed explanation, see my study, *Clothed with Power*.)

Jesus had to be on the Cross and dead by sundown on Passover because He is the paschal lamb. The exact incident had to occur by twilight and He had to be in the ground before 6 p.m. because He is the whole burnt offering sacrifice for the nation. He had to be resurrected on the third day, the day following the Sabbath, the Feast of Firstfruits, because He is the Firstfruits of the Spirit. He had to be resurrected after sunset and before sunrise. Every detail of His ordeal was laid out in the beginning through the symbolism of the feasts God ordained. God's timetable was exact. He did not deviate from it at all.

However, look at the events that put everything on this timetable.

NOW THE FESTIVAL OF UNLEAVENED BREAD, CALLED THE PASSOVER, WAS APPROACHING, AND THE CHIEF PRIESTS AND THE TEACHERS OF THE LAW WERE LOOKING FOR SOME WAY TO GET RID OF JESUS, FOR THEY WERE AFRAID OF THE PEOPLE. —LUKE 22:1–2

At exactly the right moment, Jesus' enemies began to act on their festering hatred and fear of Him. Until that moment, Jesus had always said, "My time is not yet come" (see John 2:4 and 7:6).

Because of their impatience to finish the deed before the Sabbath, they called an unorthodox meeting of the Sanhedrin. They woke Pilate, then Herod (who just happened to be in Jerusalem at that time), and finally Pilate again. A process that should have taken at least several days was railroaded through by enemies of God. Because of their manipulation of events, every event occurred exactly on God's predetermined timetable, the timetable He had planned from the beginning of time and announced early in Israel's history.

"The LORD works out everything to its proper end—even the wicked for a day of disaster" (Proverbs 16:4). Satan is nothing more than a pawn in God's hands. Between the temptation of Jesus and His Crucifixion, Satan was watching for a perfect time to carry out his own agenda. "When the devil had finished all this tempting, he left him *until an opportune time*" (Luke 4:13, author's emphasis). Now—at this exact moment—Satan sees his opportunity.

> SATAN ENTERED JUDAS . . . AND JUDAS WENT TO THE CHIEF PRIESTS AND THE OFFICERS OF THE TEMPLE GUARD AND DISCUSSED WITH THEM HOW HE MIGHT BETRAY JESUS. . . . HE . . . *WATCHED FOR AN OPPORTUNITY* TO HAND JESUS OVER TO THEM WHEN NO CROWD WAS PRESENT. —LUKE 22:3–6, AUTHOR'S EMPHASIS

Satan found the opportune time for which he had been watching. The irony is that it was God's opportune time, not Satan's.

Through every page of Scripture, God shows us His ways. He uses everything to work out His own purposes. His purpose will prevail no matter what plans are in the hearts of men. Every one of God's enemies, though they plotted and fought against His people, became the means to His end. You and I, His children who are in covenant relationship with Him, are never at the mercy of any person or any circumstance. God is never taken by surprise at any person's decisions or actions. He has already factored them in to His purpose and plan for us.

God is completely in control. Satan is acting only as God permits him to act. If the answer to your prayer will require an unbeliever to be responsive to God, remember: an unbeliever is under Satan's power, and Satan is under God's power. Therefore, even an unbeliever is under God's power. Do not fear.

Think back through your specific fears, and in each case name the

person(s) whose decisions will impact the outcome of events. As you list each name, commit that person to God, and let the truth of God's Word settle on your heart.

_____

_____

_____

_____

———————————◯———————————

Let's keep going and drill down to the very core of how God's sovereignty works. Let's pose some questions about how God has shown Himself capable and willing to act in regard to unbelievers.

Does God have the power and does He ever choose to restrain an unbeliever from committing a particular sin in a particular moment? Consider the story of Joseph. Joseph's evil brothers with malicious intent, who were not attuned to God or interested in His guidance, made a masterful, intricate plan to kill Joseph and hide their culpability. The Bible gives a condensed account in Genesis 37. Imagine how many long and involved conversations and how much individual thought must have gone into such a scheme. Joseph was likely a familiar point of conversation among them and their resentment of him likely the centerpiece of their talk. Imagine the brainstorming sessions they may have had as they created their plot, considering and then rejecting several options, and finally settling on one that seemed to have no loopholes. Evil, evil, evil.

Plotting scheming, fine-tuning the idea until they had ironed out all the wrinkles, deciding who would do what, how they might lay the trap. Though the moment occurred without their arranging it, the idea to kill their younger brother is not one likely to have occurred to them on the spur of the moment, with all the brothers in unison. Their opportunity serendipitously presented itself when Jacob sent Joseph to check on his brothers. They spotted him from a remote distance, leaving them plenty of time to put their plans into action. The Bible leaves no room to speculate on their intent:

> THEY PLOTTED AGAINST HIM TO PUT HIM TO DEATH. THEY SAID TO ONE ANOTHER, "HERE COMES THIS DREAMER! NOW THEN, COME AND LET US KILL HIM AND THROW HIM INTO ONE OF THE PITS; AND WE WILL SAY, 'A WILD BEAST DEVOURED HIM.'" —GENESIS 37:18–20 NASB

Although the brothers had every intention of killing Joseph, God did not allow it. First, God used Reuben to restrain them. "'Let us not take his life.' Reuben further said to them, 'Shed no blood. Throw him into this pit that is in the wilderness'" (v. 22 NASB). Now here comes the good part. The brothers, having thrown Joseph into the pit, sat down to eat a meal and "Behold, a caravan of Ishmaelites was coming from Gilead . . . on their way . . . down to Egypt" (v. 25 NASB). What a coincidence! Behold! Just at that moment a band of traders pass by that very spot on their way to Egypt—right where God wants Joseph.

Only then did the brothers decide not to kill Joseph.

> JUDAH SAID TO HIS BROTHERS, "WHAT PROFIT IS IT FOR US TO KILL OUR BROTHER AND COVER UP HIS BLOOD? COME AND LET US SELL HIM TO THE ISHMAELITES AND NOT LAY OUR HANDS ON HIM, FOR HE IS OUR BROTHER, OUR *OWN* FLESH." AND HIS BROTHERS LISTENED TO *HIM*. —GENESIS 37:26–27 NASB

What if the band of traders had come along earlier or later than they did? What if they had been taking another route or if the brothers had been eating their meal at another spot? What if the traders had been headed somewhere other than Egypt? What if they were of some other occupation, one not disposed to buying and selling? Behold! Everything came together in a single moment to move God's plan forward. And notice—neither the brothers nor the Ishmaelite traders were seeking God's direction.

Notice further, Reuben was the brother who initially kept Joseph from being killed. His plan was to sneak back to the pit, rescue Joseph, and return him to their father (vv. 21–22). That seems like a good and noble plan, doesn't it? But, you see, it was Reuben's plan. Well-intentioned though it was, it was not God's plan. Reuben's plan would not have accomplished God's plan. God wanted to use Joseph in Egypt. Not only did God override overtly evil plans and substitute His own plan, He also prevented a well-meant but flesh-born plan from being carried out. Only His plan would prevail. "Many are the plans in a person's heart, but it is the LORD's purpose that prevails" (Proverbs 19:21). "The mind of man plans his way, but the LORD directs his steps" (Proverbs 16:9 NASB). God's plan reached farther than simply saving Joseph's life. He was setting in motion the events that would bring our salvation to completion. Joseph, forced into Egypt, laid the groundwork for Israel to enter Egypt, set up the scenario under which Moses would emerge as liberator, and continued the line of God's people until Jesus was born.

To further the point, look at Jesus during the time that He was limited to an earth-bound frame. No matter how His enemies plotted and schemed, they were prevented from acting until the appointed time.

SO THEY WERE SEEKING TO SEIZE HIM; AND NO MAN LAID HIS HAND ON HIM, BECAUSE HIS HOUR HAD NOT YET COME. —JOHN 7:30 NASB

THESE WORDS HE SPOKE IN THE TREASURY, AS HE TAUGHT IN THE TEM-
PLE; AND NO ONE SEIZED HIM, BECAUSE HIS HOUR HAD NOT YET COME.
—JOHN 8:20 NASB

*Does God have the power, and does He ever choose to restrain
an unbeliever from committing a particular sin in a particular
moment?* The Bible is clear that the answer is yes. If God *can*, but
does not, then He *intentionally* does not restrain the unbeliever's
behavior. It is not out of God's helplessness that an unbeliever acts
in his sin, but in God's providence. Do not fear.

In the story of Joseph, notice how many details had to fall into
place at the right time and the right place. We can see this over
and over in Scripture. God directs the smallest details so that
events occur as He has ordered. **In the following Scripture
passages, circle the phrases that depict God's sovereignty, and
underline the phrases that indicate man's decisions.**

THIS MAN WAS HANDED OVER TO YOU BY GOD'S DELIBERATE PLAN AND
FOREKNOWLEDGE; AND YOU, WITH THE HELP OF WICKED MEN, PUT HIM
TO DEATH BY NAILING HIM TO THE CROSS. —ACTS 2:23

FOR TRULY IN THIS CITY THERE WERE GATHERED TOGETHER AGAINST
YOUR HOLY SERVANT JESUS, WHOM YOU ANOINTED, BOTH HEROD AND
PONTIUS PILATE, ALONG WITH THE GENTILES AND THE PEOPLES OF
ISRAEL, TO DO WHATEVER YOUR HAND AND YOUR PURPOSE PREDES-
TINED TO OCCUR. —ACTS 4:27–28 NASB

Though God does not predetermine man's actions, He does fore-
know. In foreknowing, He works man's choices into His plan and
uses them for His purposes.

Does God ever intentionally allow unbelievers to commit sinful acts in order to bring about His own ends? If He has the power to restrain unbelievers, then it is clear that many times He allows unbelievers to act seemingly without restraint. This is only the case if the unbeliever's actions will set the stage for the next step in the working out of God's purpose. The actions of an unbeliever are always, always being harnessed and held in check by God. They are never acting without restraint. The full-scale plan of the enemy is never fully being carried out.

Let's look at Joseph again. Some of his brothers' evil plans succeeded, but what did those actions set in motion?

Brother's treachery >> Ishmaelite traders >> Egypt >> Potiphar >> Potiphar's wife >> prison >> meeting with cup bearer and baker >> audience with Pharaoh >> promotion in Egypt >> provision for Israel >> Israel in Egypt >> Moses >> Passover >> Jesus.

One thing leads to the next. Each event sets the stage for the next step.

Do you see? By allowing Joseph's brothers to act out some part of their evil, God was advancing His plan. All along the way, there were moments when it appeared that Joseph's enemies acted without restraint. Yet not one single step was a false step. Every event led straight to God's goal.

Several generations before Joseph, God told Abraham that his descendants would be enslaved, but, at a specified time, would be returned to Canaan. You will find this in Genesis 15:12–16. In the course of His disclosures to Abraham, God says, "Then in the fourth generation they [Israelites] will return here, for the iniquity of the Amorite is not yet complete" (v. 16 NASB). The Amorites were the major inhabitants of Canaan. God said that He was allowing their iniquity to reach a certain measure, one He had determined, and then they would be overthrown. He was in control of how far their iniquity went. I think this is because sin must sometimes be played all the way out for the consequences to become obvious. In the middle, sin can still appear to be pleasant and easy. God would allow the Amorites to engage in their iniquity until they began to reap the results. They would be at their weakest and most vulnerable, and Israel would conquer them. Sometimes God allows a sin to be complete, reach its fullness, before He turns it around and uses it for His purpose. But He is always in control of how far it will go.

> GOD ALLOWED GODLESS MEN TO CARRY OUT THEIR PLANS. WHY? BECAUSE IT WOULD ACCOMPLISH HIS PURPOSE.

Look again at Jesus while He was in His earth body. As He approached His Crucifixion and had every appearance of being a victim of evil, He said to Pilate: "You would have no authority over Me, unless it had been given you from above" (John 19:11 NASB). Do you see that Pilate was carrying out Satan's agenda, but only because Satan was unwittingly advancing God's agenda? In Acts 2:23 we read, "This Man, delivered over by the predetermined plan and foreknowledge of God, you nailed to a cross *by the hands of godless men* and put Him to death" (NASB, author's emphasis). God allowed godless men to carry out their plans. Why? Because it would accomplish His purpose.

God is never at a loss because He cannot find someone to cooperate with Him in carrying out His plan. He so moves in the hearts of people—either Christians

or non Christians, it makes no difference—that they willingly, of their own free will carry out His plans.
—*Trusting God,* Jerry Bridges

If a situation you are praying about seems to take a wrong turn—if an unbeliever seems to be thwarting God's work—step back and get a look at the big picture. Take into account that God is managing the entire situation and that He is a micromanager. Not one small detail is lost to Him. What God is doing is, at the moment, in the invisible realm. But count on it—He is in control. Walk by faith and not by sight. Do not fear.

———————————————

Consider the circumstance that is causing you fear. Is there anything happening right now that seems to be orchestrated by the enemy?

Ask the Father to engender belief and faith. Ask Him to speak His truth into your heart about the situation so that His Word flushes out anxiety and fear. Write your prayer.

_____

_____

_____

_____

_____

_____

_____

_____

_____

Tomorrow we will tackle two more questions about how God's sovereignty operates even though man has his own free will.

THE TRUTH OF GOD
DAY FOUR

I HOPE YOU ARE RECOGNIZING THE CLEAR TEACHING OF SCRIPTURE THAT GOD IS ALWAYS IN CONTROL AND NO FORCE CAN THWART HIS PLANS AND PURPOSES. Whatever it is that you fear, God is fully in control. Let's keep asking the questions and looking to Scripture for answers.

Does God ever take the initiative to stir up the imagination of unbelievers so that they act in ways consistent with their own nature, yet bringing about God's purpose? Does God ever initiate, create, and direct the actions of unbelievers? Does He ever use their natural inclinations to set them on a particular course that will bring about His purposes?

In Exodus 1:7–11 we read how the Hebrew nation went from being a protected people in Egypt to being slaves in Egypt.

> NOW A NEW KING AROSE OVER EGYPT, WHO DID NOT KNOW JOSEPH. HE SAID TO HIS PEOPLE, "BEHOLD, THE PEOPLE OF THE SONS OF ISRAEL ARE MORE AND MIGHTIER THAN WE. COME, LET US DEAL WISELY WITH THEM, OR ELSE THEY WILL MULTIPLY AND IN THE EVENT OF WAR, THEY WILL ALSO JOIN THEMSELVES TO THOSE WHO HATE US, AND FIGHT AGAINST US AND DEPART FROM THE LAND." SO THEY APPOINTED TASKMASTERS OVER THEM TO AFFLICT THEM WITH HARD LABOR.
> —EXODUS 1:8–11 NASB

In Psalm 105:24–25 we read about the same event, this time told from heaven's perspective rather than earth's.

> AND HE CAUSED HIS PEOPLE TO BE VERY FRUITFUL, AND MADE THEM STRONGER THAN THEIR ADVERSARIES. *HE TURNED THEIR HEART*

TO HATE HIS PEOPLE, TO DEAL CRAFTILY WITH HIS SERVANTS.
—PSALM 105:24–25 NASB, AUTHOR'S EMPHASIS

God turned the Egyptians' hearts against His people. God was working out an eternal agenda, and He used the evil inclinations of the pharaoh's heart, steering him in a direction that would move events toward God's objective. "In the LORD's hand the king's heart is a stream of water that he channels toward all who please him" (Proverbs 21:1).

Some 400 years later when Moses led the Israelites out from Egypt, at the last minute the pharaoh changed his mind and decided to pursue the Israelites to bring them back. God says it happened like this: "Thus I will harden Pharaoh's heart, and he will chase after them; and I will be honored through Pharaoh and all his army . . . As for Me, behold, I will harden the hearts of the Egyptians so that they will go in after them" (Exodus 14:4, 17 NASB).

God was setting the stage for the display of His power. The Egyptians would act in ways consistent with their character; God would not turn them from being righteous to being evil, but He would use their own mind-set and inclinations and move them to take action that would provide Him with the platform He wanted. He did not impose decisions on them. He did not predetermine their choices, but He foreknew their choices and used them to His advantage.

Years passed. The Israelites entered the Promised Land under Joshua's leadership. Forty years earlier God had promised the Israelites that they would conquer the land. Now He was making good on His promise.

THERE WAS NOT A CITY WHICH MADE PEACE WITH THE SONS OF ISRAEL EXCEPT THE HIVITES LIVING IN GIBEON; THEY TOOK THEM ALL IN BATTLE. *FOR IT WAS OF THE LORD TO HARDEN THEIR HEARTS*, TO MEET ISRAEL

IN BATTLE IN ORDER THAT HE MIGHT UTTERLY DESTROY THEM, THAT THEY MIGHT RECEIVE NO MERCY, BUT THAT HE MIGHT DESTROY THEM, JUST AS THE LORD HAD COMMANDED MOSES. —JOSHUA 11:19–20 NASB, AUTHOR'S EMPHASIS

It was the Lord's doing that caused the inhabitants of the land to meet Israel in battle. Why? So that Joshua could utterly destroy them. God did not want His people making compromises with their enemies. I believe He was demonstrating His own plan for Satan and dealing with his forces. No peace treaties. No reaching an understanding. Utter, total destruction. But in order for Israel to overcome the inhabitants, they had to meet them in battle. God engineered it.

Now move with me to Isaiah 10. Israel, stubborn and unresponsive to the prophets' warnings, came under God's judgment. In verses 10–15, we read God's explanation of His acts of judgment, enacted through the pagan nation of Assyria, who God calls the "rod of My anger" (v. 5 NASB). Walk with me through these Scriptures.

WOE TO ASSYRIA, THE ROD OF MY ANGER AND THE STAFF IN WHOSE HANDS IS MY INDIGNATION, I SEND IT AGAINST A GODLESS NATION AND COMMISSION IT AGAINST THE PEOPLE OF MY FURY. —ISAIAH 10:5–6 NASB

(*Here we see God commissioning Assyria as His tool of judgment.*)

YET IT DOES NOT SO INTEND, NOR DOES IT PLAN SO IN ITS HEART, BUT RATHER IT IS ITS PURPOSE TO DESTROY AND TO CUT OFF MANY NATIONS. —ISAIAH 10:7 NASB

(*Assyria has other plans. Their purpose is to destroy many nations instead of just little Israel. In verses 12–14, the king of Assyria boasts of his victory. God then points out how ludicrous it is for Assyria to boast.)*

> IS THE AXE TO BOAST ITSELF OVER THE ONE WHO CHOPS WITH IT? IS THE SAW TO EXALT ITSELF OVER THE ONE WHO WIELDS IT? *THAT* WOULD BE LIKE A CLUB WIELDING THOSE WHO LIFT IT, OR LIKE A ROD LIFTING *HIM* WHO IS NOT WOOD. —ISAIAH 10:15 NASB

God used Assyria for His own purposes. He was in control from beginning to end. Assyria's plans did not come to fruition, but God's plan did.

When the situation you are praying about seems to be controlled by an unbeliever taking a wrong, rebellious action, God is in control. Wait it out. Watch. When it all comes together you will see—what looked wrong in the moment turned out to be necessary to the process. Do not fear.

———

Is there anything about the situation that is causing you fear right now—either real, anticipated, or imagined—in which it seems that evil is winning the day and determining the outcome?

Allow the Holy Spirit to describe it to you differently. Let Him change the narrative you have been telling yourself. Write out the situation as He sees it.

Does God ever allow a believer to operate intentionally in his or her flesh because the results will serve God's purposes and set the stage for the next step in His plan? Let's turn our attention to believers who are acting in their flesh instead of in the power of the Spirit. Can they thwart God's intentions?

We are talking here about a believer who is resisting God, who is determined to act in his flesh. We are not talking about a believer who genuinely wants to know and do God's will. God is able to move upon that believer with such irresistible power that the person will be drawn to act in accordance with the Spirit. On the other hand, when He does not do so—when He allows a believer to act in his flesh—it is because the results will serve God's purpose. Consider Simon Peter.

> SIMON, SIMON, SATAN HAS ASKED TO SIFT ALL OF YOU AS WHEAT. BUT I HAVE PRAYED FOR YOU, SIMON, THAT YOUR FAITH MAY NOT FAIL. AND WHEN YOU HAVE TURNED BACK, STRENGTHEN YOUR BROTHERS.
> —LUKE 22:31–32

Jesus tells Simon that Satan has asked permission to put him to the test. Obviously, if Satan asked permission, God could have denied him that permission. Possibly, God had denied him permission numerous times. But this time Satan was given permission to tempt Simon. God knew before the event that Simon would be defeated, in the moment, by the test. However, the Father also knew that Simon Peter would repent and turn again. His plan was to use Simon Peter's failure and subsequent repentance and restoration to strengthen other believers. Simon Peter's failure and Jesus' response to him would mark Simon Peter for the rest of his life. Through Simon Peter's fall into temptation, God would be able to accomplish and teach things He could not have if Simon Peter had never fallen.

There will be times when God, working out the process of His will, allows a believer to fall. When you are praying about a situation and you see this principle at work, you can be certain that God is in control. You can rest in the fact that He is in the process of working out a great and eternal plan. You can trust that this bump in the road really is His sovereignty in operation. Do not fear.

Does God ever use His intervening power to stop a believer who is determined to act in his or her flesh? If God, in working out His purposes, sometimes allows a believer to intentionally act in his or her flesh, then does He sometimes stop a believer who is determined to act in his or her flesh? Consider the story of Balaam in Numbers 22:22–35. Read the whole account so you can get this in its proper context.

Balaam is a prophet of the Lord. King of the Moabites, Balak, wants to hire Balaam to curse the Israelites. At the point we take up this story, Balaam has told the men from Balak that he will retire for the night and see what God will say to him. "God came to Balaam at night and said to him, 'If the men have come to call you, rise up and go with them; but only the word which I speak to you shall you do'" (Numbers 22:20 NASB). The next morning, Balaam did not wait to see if the men would come to call him. Instead he saddled up his donkey and set out (v. 21). God was angry with him because he was going and sent an angel to intercept him forcefully on his way. "But God was angry because he was going, and the angel of the LORD took his stand in the way as an adversary against him. . . . The angel of the LORD said to him . . . 'Behold, I have come out as an adversary, because your way was contrary to me'" (Numbers 22:22, 32 NASB).

God has the power to intervene in the affairs of a believer who is acting in the flesh with such force as to stop him or her in his or her tracks. If this is what is necessary for putting God's will into place, then this is exactly what God will do. Otherwise, He is intentionally not intervening to stop the action. Do not fear.

LINE UPON LINE

As we build the case line upon line, are you more convinced that there is no force that can prevail against God's good plan? Does faith that is grounded in the truth begin to tame fear that is engendered by a lie? When you pray the prayer of faith under the leadership of the Spirit, do not let your faith be shaken—do not fall into fear—when circumstances take a turn that seems wrong to you at the moment. The power of God is fully able to accomplish all that needs to be accomplished to bring about the fitting conclusion. Wait it out. His plans are for good and not for evil. His plans are to give you a future and a hope. Nothing can keep God from being able to do all that He intends to do. "For the LORD Almighty has purposed, and who can thwart him? His hand is stretched out, and who can turn it back?" (Isaiah 14:27). "Who can speak and have it happen if the Lord has not decreed it?" (Lamentations 3:37). Author Jerry Bridges says in his book *Trusting God*:

> Confidence in the sovereignty of God in all that affects us is crucial to our trusting Him. If there is a single event in all of the universe that can occur outside of God's sovereign control then we cannot trust Him. His love may be infinite, but if His power is limited and His purpose can be thwarted, we cannot trust Him.

Bringing these scriptural truths to bear on your specific fear(s),

next to these statements, write "I believe." Add the date.

———————— All God's plans for me and those I love are for good, and God has no plan for me or for those I love that is not loving and beneficial.

———————— God knows what I do not, and He is acting in accordance with His wisdom and knowledge.

———————— Nothing can thwart God's purposes or plans.

———————— I choose to trust God and let faith tame my fear.

THE PRESENCE OF GOD

WE HAVE DIVED IN DEEP THIS WEEK AND WRESTLED WITH SOME MISCONCEPTIONS THAT MIGHT KEEP US FROM BEING ABLE TO FULLY REST IN GOD'S SOVEREIGNTY. I hope you have reached the conclusion that because of God's love, He desires what is best. Because of His wisdom, He knows what is best. Because of His power, He can bring about what is best. We have nothing to fear.

To fight fear, we feed faith. To weed out worry, we cultivate our intimate relationship with the God who loves us beyond reason. Only by knowing Him and deepening our understanding of Him will we have firm ground on which to stand when we face our enemy's lies and say, "Of whom shall I be afraid?"

Commenting on Psalm 27:1, Alexander Maclaren says: "Only he who can say, 'The Lord is the strength of my life' can say, 'Of whom shall I be afraid?'" God has come near to us and has made Himself knowable so that we have access to His heart and mind.

As we close out this week's study material, let me call your attention to Psalm 34:4. "I sought the LORD, and he answered me; he delivered me from all my fears." David declares that the Lord delivered him from his fears. He did not say yet that he had been delivered from what caused his fear. We can navigate life, with all its harsh realities and frightful possibilities, without being held captive to fear. Fear does not have to run the show. We can look life's situations in the eye and still say, "Whom shall I fear?" When we know God, and understand His heart toward us, there is nothing left that we have to fear.

FEARLESS

THE LORD IS MY LIGHT AND MY SALVATION—WHOM SHALL I FEAR? THE
LORD IS THE STRONGHOLD OF MY LIFE—OF WHOM SHALL I BE AFRAID?
—PSALM 27:1

David, as he penned this psalm, was surrounded by enemies who
were set on his destruction. His circumstances were grim. He
had good reason to fear. Yet, he did not fear. He was aware of his
situation. He was realistic about his conditions. He could look
reality in the eye and not blink. He realized that his circumstances were set pieces on God's stage. He knew that the action was
under God's direction. He defined his situation in terms of God's
protection instead of in terms of his exposure to danger. That's
what held his attention. He had already learned what the writer
of Hebrews taught generations later: "We do this by keeping our
eyes on Jesus, the champion who initiates and perfects our faith"
(Hebrews 12:2 NLT).

Your mind always needs a reference point to correctly see reality. For example, imagine looking at a photograph of an object that
fills the frame. It looks big. Then you see a photograph of that same
object, but held in a person's hand. Now, with the hand as a reference point, your perception of the object's size changes. Or, imagine
that you are in a traffic jam and all around you are big trucks that
obscure your view of the horizon. If the trucks begin to move, it
will feel as though you are the one moving. When your horizon
comes back in view, you reorient and know that you are sitting still.
The horizon is your reference point. Without a reference point, your
perceptions are skewed. Jesus invites us to make His presence our
one and only reference point. Fix your eyes on Him. When our eyes
are locked on Jesus, His presence is our reality. Nothing else seems

so compelling or so worthy of attention. His face fills our frame of reference and everything else pales.

Do you have some circumstances that give you good reason to fear? Let the eyes of your heart come to rest on the God who shelters and protects you, who fights for you. Let Him be your frame of reference.

Right now, consider again the things you identified as your fears. Take time to soak in His presence and respond to His nearness. When you fix your eyes on Jesus and let Him be your reference point, how does that change what you observe? Write out any thoughts or reflections.

_____

_____

_____

_____

_____

_____

ALL MY FEARS

Fear comes in many variations. As the study progresses, we'll look at many of those variations and specific remedies. But right now let's focus on the fact that the Word promises that He can free you from every kind of fear. David says in Psalm 34:4, "He delivered me from all my fears." Notice that later in the psalm David says that God had delivered him from all his troubles (v. 6), but first David reflects on the way that God delivered him from his fears.

Why does God repeat His injunction, "Do not fear," over and over? Because there is much to fear. He does not promise to give you a life that has nothing fearful in it, but He does promise to buffer you in such a way that fear does not have the last word. We don't have to give fear free rein in our lives. We are not at the mercy of events outside us because we have the living, present, fearless Jesus inside us.

> Every new duty calls for more grace than I now possess,
> but not more than is found in thee,
> the divine Treasury in whom all fullness dwells.
>
> To thee I repair for grace upon grace,
> until every void made by sin be replenished
> and I am filled with all thy fullness.
>
> —"Grace Active," *The Valley of Vision: A Collection of Puritan Prayers & Devotions*

You have already been delivered from all your fears by the very presence of the Overcomer Himself. He's there, waiting for you to lean into Him. To rest the weight of your fears and worries on Him. Your fears and worries are heavy to you, but weightless to Him. There He is. Do not fear.

Take some time right now to ponder the wonderful truth that Jesus lives in you. Right now. Right here. In the middle of your fear and worry, there He is. Just be still, and know that He is present and He is God.

Is there anything about your fear-inducing situation that is too big for Jesus to handle?

_____

_____

Now listen to Him speak this to your heart:

BE STRONG AND COURAGEOUS. DO NOT BE AFRAID OR TERRIFIED BECAUSE OF THEM, FOR THE LORD YOUR GOD GOES WITH YOU; HE WILL NEVER LEAVE YOU NOR FORSAKE YOU. —DEUTERONOMY 31:6

I AM WITH YOU AND WILL WATCH OVER YOU WHEREVER YOU GO, AND I WILL BRING YOU BACK TO THIS LAND. I WILL NOT LEAVE YOU UNTIL I HAVE DONE WHAT I HAVE PROMISED YOU. —GENESIS 28:15

AND SURELY I AM WITH YOU ALWAYS, TO THE VERY END OF THE AGE. —MATTHEW 28:20

What difference does it make to you that Jesus is present for you in all His power in whatever situation you face? Write your response to Him.

_____

_____

_____

_____

_____

_____

_____

_____

_____

Next week we will begin to look at the very practical ways that God wants us to learn to navigate fear as we examine the process that God is using to free us from all our fears.

THE PROCESS OF OF PRAYER

As you are learning to live a praying life, prayer takes on a much broader definition than "saying prayers." Much of what prayer is accomplishing cannot be condensed to a list. Many times the direct answers to petitions are the least important aspect of what the prayer accomplished. I believe that as you progress and mature into a praying life, your testimony of prayer's effectiveness will be that the mercies of God unfold at every turn. You walk in answered prayer. O. Hallesby states it like this:

> The longer you live a life of this kind, the more answers to prayer you will experience. As white snowflakes fall quietly and thickly on a winter's day, answers to prayer will settle down upon you at every step you take, even to your dying day.

It is during the process of prayer that God does His mightiest work. If this were not so, then God would have set prayer up to work like a vending machine: put in a request, get out an answer. God has a loving and productive reason for the process of prayer.

—*Live a Praying Life*®

THE EFFECT OF FEAR
DAY ONE

GOD HAS ARRANGED PRAYER IN SUCH A WAY THAT IT IS A PROCESS, RATHER THAN A ONE-AND-DONE, STOP-AND-GO AFFAIR. In a praying life, we are giving God full access to every part of our lives and our personalities so that He can work in the deepest recesses of our hearts and minds.

He has orderly ways that He works. He has a strategy. We come to Him in prayer with one thing on our minds, and He takes that one thing and begins to work in layers and at depths we had not imagined. Open your life to Him, and He will take it from there. Your precise struggle or need in this precise moment is His entry point. We want our situation fixed; He wants our souls healed.

As we consider fear and worry in particular, let's get specific about understanding the process of being set free from fear's clutches.

THE EXPERIENCE OF FEAR

The way you experience fear might be like a continual battle. Some people struggle with fear on a daily basis. Fear and worry might be your normal. For you, it is likely that most of your experience of fear is about things that might happen but haven't. Your mind naturally goes to the most dire possibility.

Maybe you experience fear and worry about things that might happen, but not continually. Perhaps there are certain topics—children, health, or finances—that draw you into fear and worry.

Perhaps you are struggling with fear or worry right now because you are facing a real-time situation that presents fearful possibilities. Maybe the very thing you feared has occurred, and you are struggling to stay afloat and not get sucked into the vortex of worry and anxiety.

You might define your struggle differently and not call it fear. Maybe you struggle with anger. Did you realize that fear fuels anger? Think about it. Why did you feel angry in a given situation? Did you fear losing some control? Being exposed? Not being enough? Being seen as a failure? Being proved wrong?

Maybe you struggle with feeling depressed or discouraged. I'm not addressing clinical depression or brain chemistry-related situations. These are real and physical and need professional attention. I'm talking about a negative mind-set and general feeling of discouragement that is occasional and perhaps triggered by events or situations.

It is likely that fear is the bedrock of such feelings. Fear and worry overwhelm you, and you cycle into expecting the worst. You are likely to infect those around you with your gloom.

Maybe you struggle with compulsive behaviors like overeating or overspending. What drives these behaviors? Possibly fear. You might use them to avoid what you fear to confront.

Fear expresses itself in our lives in countless ways. It is such a well-used game plan concocted by your spiritual enemy, whose end game is to "kill, steal, and destroy" (John 10:10), that God counters it over and over and over and over. He already knows that fear is where our minds default, and so He opens the conversation with, "Do not fear." (For example, Isaiah 41:10; 43:1; Joshua 1:9; Deuteronomy 31:6. In fact, He exhorts us not to be afraid numerous times and in a variety of circumstances in Scripture.)

How are you experiencing fear right now?

_____

_____

_____

When you let fear have its way, what do you realize it is stealing from you? What is it killing and destroying?

_____

_____

_____

Would you agree that if your goal were to kill, steal, and destroy, inciting fear would be the way to go?

_____

_____

Satan keeps using fear because fear works. He knows how to aim it squarely at his mark. He is not in you because Jesus is in residence, but he knows very well how to manipulate you from the outside, pouncing on your every weakness and introducing fear into your thoughts. He never misses an opportunity. He watches and waits. Scheming. Peter describes him, in 1 Peter 5:8, as a hungry lion, on the hunt. Attention focused. Anticipating his kill.

THE EFFECT OF FEAR

Your enemy wants to diminish your life, steal your joy, destroy your peace, and kill your relationships and even your body by his skillful use of fear as a weapon. Jesus wants just the opposite for you. He wants you to live fearlessly and exuberantly, safe in His care.

Every single thing Jesus wants to give you, fear is designed to steal. Fear targets joy and peace like a heat-seeking missile. God did not devise fear. "For the Spirit God gave us does not make us timid, but gives us power, love and self-discipline" (2 Timothy 1:7). Fear or timidity does not come from God. Then where does it come from? It is a result of the fall and a natural by-product of human sin. It's a tool that Satan manipulates for his own purposes—to kill, steal, and destroy. To counter with perfect precision the peace and joy Jesus offers. Satan engineered it. He wired it and knows exactly how it works best and how to make the best use of it.

So, consider: Fear is from the father of lies, the evil one. Satan has no weapon to use against us other than the weapon of lies. He has no material with which to construct his weapons other than lies. Truth is not in him—he has only lies that he can use to manipulate us and draw us into fear. Conclusion? Fear is a lie. (Let me repeat what I said at the beginning. We are not dealing with healthy fear meant to protect us, but instead the fear that comes from believing the lies the enemy wants to use.)

What lie does fear tell us? It always tells us *God is not*. What has God told us is His name? I AM. Fear says *God is not*: He is not good, He is not able, He is not willing, He is not faithful, He is not loving, He is not on your side.

What is your fear telling you right now?

_____

_____

_____

_____

What is I AM telling you about Himself?

_____

_____

_____

_____

_____

Which do you choose to embrace? Right now, let me suggest a little commitment ceremony. It is not magical or mystical, and if you don't feel comfortable with it, don't do it. It won't give your prayers more power or influence God in any way. But, if you want to, just put your fingers on top of the words you wrote that God is telling you about Himself and tell God and your enemy, "This is the truth I receive and embrace." Add the date next to the entry.

If our enemy is watchful, waiting for his opportune moment, then certainly we should be watchful. We should be on the lookout and ready to jump out of his reach. When Peter describes him as a roaring lion, he says this: "Be alert [watchful, vigilant] and of sober mind [clear thinking]. Your enemy the devil prowls around like a roaring lion looking for someone to devour" (1 Peter 5:8). Colossians 4:2 uses the same word to tell us to stay on the watch, and again in 1 Corinthians 16:13 to be "on your guard." Ephesians 6:18 tells us to be "alert," a word that means to keep vigilant watch over.

Your enemy is clever, but he is no match for Jesus in you. As soon as his schemes are revealed, they prove to be trite and tired. Overused. During this study, we are going to discover how to deal with the enemy's old, tired maneuvers so that we can live in the freedom and joy that is ours in Jesus.

DAY TWO
THE PURVEYOR OF FEAR

SATAN DOES NOT CHANGE. His purposes don't change. His weapons don't change. His tactics don't change. He has plans. In 2 Corinthians 2:11 Paul refers to the enemy's "schemes." The word means his strategy, his well-thought-out plan. In Ephesians 6:11 Paul again refers to Satan's "schemes." Here the word means a crafty scheme meant to deceive.

Read Genesis 3:1–6:

> NOW THE SERPENT WAS MORE CRAFTY [SHREWD, SKILLFUL, TRICKY, SUBTLE] THAN ANY OF THE WILD ANIMALS THE LORD GOD HAD MADE. HE SAID TO THE WOMAN, "DID GOD REALLY SAY, 'YOU MUST NOT EAT FROM ANY TREE IN THE GARDEN'?" THE WOMAN SAID TO THE SERPENT, "WE MAY EAT FRUIT FROM THE TREES IN THE GARDEN, BUT GOD DID SAY, 'YOU MUST NOT EAT FRUIT FROM THE TREE THAT IS IN THE MIDDLE OF THE GARDEN, AND YOU MUST NOT TOUCH IT, OR YOU WILL DIE.'" "YOU WILL NOT CERTAINLY DIE," THE SERPENT SAID TO THE WOMAN. "FOR GOD KNOWS THAT WHEN YOU EAT FROM IT YOUR EYES WILL BE OPENED, AND YOU WILL BE LIKE GOD, KNOWING GOOD AND EVIL." WHEN THE WOMAN SAW THAT THE FRUIT OF THE TREE WAS GOOD FOR FOOD AND PLEASING TO THE EYE, AND ALSO DESIRABLE FOR GAINING WISDOM, SHE TOOK SOME AND ATE IT.

How is Satan described? Or, what is his primary characteristic?

_____

_____

What did he hint to Eve about God? Or, what about God's nature did he skillfully introduce into her thoughts?

_____

_____

_____

_____

Do you recognize where he introduced fear? If it doesn't pop out for you, let me elaborate.

———————◯———————

What I want us to see here is that Satan's tactics do not change. He's just not that creative, and he doesn't have any wiggle room. He's an exceptional liar, but that's his limit. As we know the Truth—Jesus Himself—better and better, the enemy's lies are less effective. With that in mind, let's unpack this very familiar story and look for some fresh insight.

SNAKE OIL SALESMAN

Notice how wily Satan is in his approach. He can't really approach Eve directly with accusations against God because she knows Him, walks with Him, and has never doubted Him. He has to introduce doubt subtly. That's his first step. To God's I AM, Satan has to suggest _God is not_. And he sidles in like the con artist he is. Not a head-on assault, but a sneaky approach that does not set off alarm bells. Sounds very reasonable. Worth a listen.

I wonder about the tone of the conversation. I can hear it two ways, either of which would be characteristic of Satan and effective to produce his outcome.

First, hear him say this in a conspiratorial whispery voice. "Did God really say that? Why would He say that? I guess because He knows that if you eat, you'll be like Him! Hard to believe He'd want to deprive you of that." Casting doubt on God's intentions toward her.

Second version. Hear this with a condescending tone. "Are you sure that's what He said? Are you sure you heard Him correctly? Because that doesn't make sense. You won't die!" he says sarcastically, mockingly. "Who would believe that you'll die just for eating from this perfectly lovely tree? What's it here for if not to eat from? You won't die. Far from it. You'll know good and evil, just like God. Surely that is not what He meant." Casting doubt on her understanding of what God said. Encouraging her to evaluate the situation in light of her best understanding instead of taking God at His word.

Either way. Both ways. He gets her ear. She starts to listen to a voice other than God's. So, little niggles of fear and insecurity begin to invade her mind. What if God intends to withhold something that would make her happier? What if she is confused about what God said? All this time she had been living her life as if God were only good and completely loving, wanting her to enjoy the life He had given her. All this time, she had been acting as if God meant what He said and as if His commands were for her protection. Maybe she had been fooled. Maybe God was holding something back.

> IN THE END, THE FEAR THAT IS INTRODUCED FROM THE BEGINNING IS THIS: FEAR OF MISSING OUT.

Now, Eve has transferred her trust from the Solid Rock to her own perceptions and best ideas. Intrinsically, she knows that her trust is now on shaky ground. Life is suddenly a little more precarious than she first thought.

In the end, the fear that is introduced from the beginning is this: fear of missing out. Think about it. Every fear or worry you have identified in your life right now, you fear missing something that you think would make you happy. Fear that maybe God will withhold His best, probably because you aren't worth His best. You deserve to be deprived.

In each fear or worry, is this not true? You have an "if only" prayer. "If only this will happen, or that won't happen, or this will change, or that won't change . . . then everything will be fine and I'll be happy and secure."

—————————

Think about your particular fears and worries. Be ruthlessly honest. We're all in this battle together. Invite the Holy Spirit to reveal whatever needs to be revealed.

Are you fearful that God might withhold the very best outcome from you?

_____

Are you fearful that God might not be true to His Word in your case?

_____

What do you fear being deprived of?

_____

_____

What is your "if only" prayer?

_____

_____

_____

_____

FEAR AT WORK

Fear sneaks in. It doesn't just show up out of nowhere. We are born with a readiness to learn fear. From the day we are born—fearful of nothing other than falling—fear grows. We've already acknowledged that some fear plays a protective role and when the fear is authentic, it is God's gift. We are talking about the development of false fear. Along with the real fear, false fears begin to find a home.

Fear of falling would be a legitimate fear, and would serve a protective purpose. Yet, even that fear can morph into false fear. Years ago, I remember reading a study from a group of scientists who were studying the rate at which the physical senses mature. They conducted an experiment in which they studied the depth perception of crawling babies who were placed on a flat, level floor that was a black and white checkerboard pattern. At a certain place in the floor, the black and white alternating squares became progressively smaller giving the visual illusion of a sudden steep drop-off. None of the babies would come near the place they perceived as the edge.

As I read this report, I thought, *how like us.* These babies were acting on their immature, uninformed perceptions of reality. Because they did not know about optical illusions, their activity was limited and restricted to a small area, when in reality they had a large space in which to safely play. If only they had known the truth, they would have been free to expand their horizons; but they are immature and cannot make judgments based on anything except appearance.

So, real fear becomes false fear, and instead of trusting God's reality, we pull into ourselves and develop protections we don't need and zero in on our doubts so that fear starts calling the shots. It seems that our human nature, apart from the redeeming, restoring work of Christ in us, is hard wired for fear. When challenges appear, we default to fear. Fear is our habit.

When fear runs the show, our world shrinks. Our options seem limited. Our boundaries are tight. Fear binds us and inhibits us and chains us to the wall. Remember, fear was carefully designed by your enemy to accomplish his purpose to kill, steal, and destroy.

———

For a minute, just let your imagination run free. Refer back to your childhood. Remember how you could imagine without any restrictions? If you did not have to fear failure, lack, or the opinions of others, what would you do? It doesn't have to be something realistic or even spiritual. Just exercise your imagination the way it used to work. For fun.

DAY THREE
THE HABIT OF FEAR

FEAR IS A HABIT. It has been ingrained in our brains by repetition. We default to fear. Maybe you don't default to fear in every challenge, but there are areas of challenge where you find yourself in fear mode before you have time to reason a response.

Let's look at habit. *Merriam-Webster's* dictionary defines *habit* as "an acquired mode of behavior that has become nearly or completely involuntary." See? No thinking required. Automated. A very great deal of our lives are lived by habit, which is not a bad thing, just a true thing. It only becomes bad or harmful when those habits are destructive, like fear. The book *The Power of Habit* by Charles Duhigg references a paper published by a Duke University researcher in 2006 that found more than 40 percent of the actions people performed each day weren't actually decisions but habits.

Every habit starts out as a decision and by repetition becomes habit. Habits are beneficial. Because I tend to be a scattered person, over my life I have developed a habit of putting certain things in the same place every time I lay them down. Otherwise, I waste time looking for them. Car keys, bills, sunglasses . . . each goes to its appointed place, and I never change that place. Now I don't ever have to think about it. I developed that habit on purpose because I saw its advantage. Other habits seem to have slipped in unnoticed. I tend to do the same things the same way when I get in my car, when I get out of bed in the morning, when getting ready for bed in the evening. All through the day, as much as I tend to be a make-it-up-as-I-go-along kind of person, most of my activities are run by habit.

There's no real reason for many habits, but habits just develop. Isn't that true of you?

Because we can recognize habits, we can change habits. As we understand that default mode, we can interrupt it and override it with new habits. It seems that we are programmed for habits. I think we will see that a habit of faith can replace our habit of fear.

HABITUAL FEAR

Habits are developed by repetition. Brain scans show that while a person is learning a new skill—think a toddler learning to walk or a teenager learning to drive—the brain is active all over. Once that action has been learned and habituated, as the action is going on, the brain becomes almost inactive. Only the part of the brain known as the basal ganglia, where automated procedures are managed, is active, and the parts of the brain where new skills are learned or where decisions are made become inactive.

Fear is something different from a skill to learn, yet fear is learned. Our brains seem to work by turning everything possible into an automatic response. We internalize the activity. Perhaps because it saves energy and effort. In *The Power of Habit*, the author explains it this way: "This process—in which the brain converts a sequence of actions into an automatic routine—is known as 'chunking,' and it's at the root of how habits form."

We have learned to default to fear. It didn't just happen, but we learned it in such a way that we didn't know we were developing a habit. You may have had the fear habit for so long that you can't remember not being fearful. Or you may have developed some of your fear habits after experiencing something fearful. When I was 19 years old, my perfectly healthy, robust, athletic brother was diagnosed with leukemia and passed away a year later. When my sons had certain ordinary, kid symptoms, I defaulted to fear that those symptoms presaged something grim. Maybe you can pinpoint where a fear habit started, and maybe you can't. It doesn't matter. You weren't born with it. It started somewhere.

A habit is activated by a cue, then a routine is set in motion that produces a reward or outcome in the form of a feeling your brain recognizes and has come to expect. Finally, decision-making shuts down. Thus, a "habit loop" is created. I know it's hard to define fear and worry as a reward, but rethink the concept of reward. It becomes familiar. We get it. It's known.

From cue through routine to reward is a series of automatic neurological connections, each step along the way fires the next neuron, then the next until a roadway called a neural pathway is built so that from cue to conclusion you are unaware of the process. The more often you travel that road, the more automatic it becomes. In *The Power of Habit*, Duhigg continues saying, "So unless you deliberately *fight* a habit—unless you find new routines—the pattern will unfold automatically." The cue has created a neurological craving. Your brain craves the familiar feeling. I know you don't feel as if you crave the place of fear or worry. You don't crave it like you might crave a brownie or an afternoon nap. But the phenomenon of craving refers to a neurological response.

Now I'm going to speculate for a minute. Here's what I think, and I'm no expert in brain function or understanding fear. I just ponder this, and here is how it seems to me: How does fear or worry become a reward? We have to feel some affinity with it, or we wouldn't default to it over and over. Do you think that at some level when we fear, we feel that it gives us some kind of control or at least input? Does it in some way feel more familiar and fitting to our human nature to be skeptical of just handing over the reins? What do you think?

————————————

Do you recognize the habit loop when it comes to your fears and worries?

_____

_____

_____

Can you identify some cues? You may not be able to right now, but think on it.

_____

_____

_____

When you are in fear or worry mode, and perhaps someone tries to redirect your thoughts, do you keep pulling back to the fear place? Is fear mode somehow more familiar than faith mode in that moment?

_____

_____

_____

What do you think about fearing being a neurological craving? Why do we keep going there if there is no payoff for it?

_____

A NEW THING

SEE, I AM DOING A NEW THING! NOW IT SPRINGS UP; DO YOU NOT
PERCEIVE IT? I AM MAKING A WAY IN THE WILDERNESS AND STREAMS
IN THE WASTELAND. —ISAIAH 43:19

Fear is a wilderness and a wasteland. Nothing thrives there. It is
relentless and scorching and barren. To rescue us, God promises
to do a new thing. To make a new road. The strongly entrenched
neural pathway that leads us automatically to fear and worry will be
laid waste and a new road (neural pathway) will be created—a road
that leads automatically to faith.

I think this is very exciting. God created your brain in such a
way that it can create new neural pathways to compensate for envi-
ronmental, behavioral, and neural changes like injury or disease.
Scientists call it neuroplasticity. It means your brain is changeable.
It can, to a degree, be remolded. When we decide to change our
minds, God can change our brains. We'll start here:

FOR IN HIM [JESUS] ALL THINGS WERE CREATED: THINGS IN HEAVEN AND
ON EARTH, VISIBLE AND INVISIBLE, WHETHER THRONES OR POWERS OR
RULERS OR AUTHORITIES; ALL THINGS HAVE BEEN CREATED THROUGH HIM
AND *FOR HIM.* —COLOSSIANS 1:16, AUTHOR'S EMPHASIS

Everything created—which includes everything in the material
realm as well as in the spiritual realm other than the Godhead—was
created *for Him.* Psalm 119:91 explains it in these words: "all things
serve you." Every single thing exists to serve His purposes. When
He created, He structured His creation so that it would be useful to

Him for accomplishing His purposes. He created your brain so that its functionality is of use to Him for healing and for bringing peace and joy in place of fear and worry.

He does the heavy lifting. We are incapable of making lasting, real change in ourselves. But we do have a part to play. We will need to cooperate with His ways and His plans for forging new pathways in our brains—pathways that lead to faith rather than fear, worship rather than worry, calm rather than chaos.

This process is not instant, it is progressive. The stronger the habit loop, the longer it may take. It bears repeating that God is doing the changing, and we are cooperating with His processes. Trust Him to make the changes as we lean into Him.

> He alone is able to replenish our hearts which the world
> has agitated and intoxicated but never been able to fill.
> —*A Guide to True Peace*

The goal is for us to live with our souls fully in a state of rest in Him, confident of His love, wisdom, Word, and power. To get to that state of rest, we will have to put forth determined effort. I know it sounds contradictory, but observe what the Word of God says.

"Come to me, all you who are weary and burdened, and I will give you rest" (Matthew 11:28). The Greek words translated "give rest" mean "to cause to cease." Jesus, Jewish rabbi that He was, no doubt was referencing the Hebrew concept of rest, laid out in God's Sabbath command. The Hebrew word for *Sabbath* means "to be finished." God finished His work, so He rested. He did not just take a break. "By the seventh day God *had finished the work* he had been doing; so on the seventh day *he rested* from all his work" (Genesis 2:2, author's emphasis). The *Theological Wordbook of the Old*

Testament says the word translated "rest," when transitive, means "to sever, put an end to," and, when intransitive, "to desist, to come to an end."

The rest to which we are invited means an end to our work. He takes on all the responsibility for bringing the needed change, but we have to come to Him. We have to put ourselves in the position for receiving that rest, and as the writer of Hebrews suggests: "make every effort to enter that rest" (Hebrews 4:11). The reason that our part of the equation starts out feeling like effort is because we will be resisting old patterns. We will be using our Christ-surrendered, Spirit-empowered will and determination to actively

> WE WILL LEARN, UNDER HIS TUTELAGE, TO NAVIGATE THE PRESENT MOMENT DIFFERENTLY.

resist the habit loop. We will be intentional about coming to Jesus, time and time again, when the old neural pathways try to suck us in. We will learn, under His tutelage, to navigate the present moment differently. To let Him sculpt a new landscape for our minds.

Are you ready for a new thing?

———

Factoring in the way that God created your brain, which is the hardware that runs the software called your "mind," what new things do these familiar verses say to you? Write out what God's living, active Word is saying to you in this moment about your particular struggle with fear or worry.

BE RENEWED IN THE SPIRIT OF YOUR MIND. —EPHESIANS 4:23 NASB

_____

_____

_____

DO NOT CONFORM TO THE PATTERN OF THIS WORLD, BUT BE TRANSFORMED BY THE RENEWING OF YOUR MIND. THEN YOU WILL BE ABLE TO TEST AND APPROVE WHAT GOD'S WILL IS—HIS GOOD, PLEASING AND PERFECT WILL.
—ROMANS 12:2

_____

_____

_____

_____

_____

DAY FOUR
THE END OF FEAR

GOD WANTS TO RENEW YOUR MIND—TO MAKE YOUR MIND BRAND NEW. He wants to change your mind by changing your brain. He wants to give your thoughts a new highway by which to travel so that your thoughts arrive at the right location. He wants to create highways that lead to the Promised Land, where there is rest for your soul.

> AND A HIGHWAY WILL BE THERE; IT WILL BE CALLED THE WAY OF HOLINESS; IT WILL BE FOR THOSE WHO WALK ON THAT WAY. THE UNCLEAN WILL NOT JOURNEY ON IT; WICKED FOOLS WILL NOT GO ABOUT ON IT. —ISAIAH 35:8

We are going to cooperate with Him in this venture. Are the following statements true of you? "Whatever my part is, I'm ready. I'm finished building my own roads that only lead me to wilderness and desert. I want You to build the roads, where You will lead me beside still waters and make me lie down in green pastures."

Are you with me? Who knows where this adventure will land us? Who knows what life will be like when we are set free from fear and worry and replace that misspent energy with full-throttle faith?

Where do we go from here? What is the first step? First, absolute surrender of every person, situation, and possession where fear or worry have any place or that you have identified as a cue.

I like ceremonies. I like tangible. I'm going to suggest a ceremony

of surrender to you. Again, the only purpose this serves is for you. God instituted ceremonies to help us grasp more fully the realities of the spiritual realm. So, don't do this if you don't want to, but do find a way to sit and listen to the Holy Spirit and fully surrender ownership and control of everyone and everything He brings to mind. You might want to share this ceremony with someone else who is on this journey with you. You might want to share it as a group.

1. Listening to the Spirit, list each person, situation, and possession He brings to mind. You've been doing this all along—be specific about your fears and worries. But listen.

2. Identify an item to represent each person, situation, or possession. This item might be a picture, a letter someone wrote you, a drawing from your child or grandchild, a dollar bill or a voided deposit slip, or a written word on a scrap of paper. Use whatever speaks to you.

3. Find a container to place your items in during this ceremony. This could be a large envelope, box, or other container that you might keep in sight. Write *Surrendered* or *Yours* on it.

4. Be open and honest before the Lord as you discuss the people, situations, and possessions that cause you fear. Tell Him about your struggle to let go. Tell Him that you know He's faithful. Just be present to Him, and know that He is present to you. Be present to the Presence. And see what transpires between you.

5. As you discuss each fear with the Lord, place that symbolic item in your container. Maybe you sing as you lay each down. Let it be meaningful to you, whatever that means for your personality.

If you want to do this as a group, I suggest that you do the listening, praying, heart surrender now, and when you gather as a group, have the ceremony together. Talk to each other about your surrender. Share the most meaningful surrender. Lay your offerings down all at once together or one by one. You do it your way.

Use all your study time today to do this. Take all the time you need.

DAY FIVE
THE REFRAMING OF FEAR

LET'S START WITH THE POWER OF WORDS. You already know the powerful effect words can have. So much so that God puts it like this: "The tongue has the power of life and death, and those who love it will eat its fruit" (Proverbs 18:21). We think more often about the effect of one person's words on another, but did you know that your negative words to yourself have a physiological and neural effect on your brain, and that means your thoughts are impacted, and that means your beliefs are formed, and that means you are on that neural pathway to fear and worry?

Remember that you might have realized that some attitudes and responses—such as anger or depression—have fear as their base. As we continue this discussion, don't discount emotions you have not previously classified as fear.

Let me introduce you to the part of your brain known as the amygdala. The amygdala is the portion of your brain that is responsible for storing the emotions associated with memory, which affects the way your brain processes memories, reactions, and decisions. I'm going to show you how the words you say to yourself—the thoughts your brain hears—have huge impact. God created your brain this way, and that is why His Word is full of instruction about how to use words with care.

Of course, words spoken to you have the same impact, as do words you speak to another. But you have no control over what others say to you. You only have control of what comes from your mouth or mind, so that is where we will focus. We are looking for what we need to do to position ourselves for God to renew us in the spirit of our minds.

Andrew Newberg and Mark Robert Waldman, in their book *Words Can Change Your Brain*, make the scientific case that "the ways we choose to use our words can improve the neural functioning of the brain." They carefully explain, with all the attendant research and verifications, what I am about to summarize briefly.

Our brains need a huge amount of energy to function because their functions are so complex. It takes even more energy to purposefully create new neural pathways, but it can be done. So, as we set out on this rewiring journey, expect it to take effort up front.

I believe words play an important part because our brain understands in words. When we are exposed to negative words—through others, in our own thoughts, either hearing them or reading them—the authors say that an MRI "would record, in less than a second, a substantial increase of activity in your amygdala and the release of dozens of stress-producing hormones and neurotransmitters. These chemicals immediately interrupt the normal functioning of your brain, especially those that are involved with logic, reason, language processing, and communication."

According to *Who Switched Off My Brain?* by Dr. Caroline Leaf, fear actually triggers a series of chemical secretions and activates the release of hormones and neurotransmitters, and, if left unchecked, this negative stimulation can cause toxic neurochemical waste to build up. If you stay in that place of negativity and fear, your brain is soaking in toxins. Fearful, negative thoughts grow other negative thoughts. Neuroscientists call it "mood congruent memory." It means that whatever emotional state you are in, the brain more easily retrieves thoughts, ideas, and memories congruent with that mood. Here is how the Scripture describes it: "When my anxious thoughts multiply within me" (Psalm 94:19 NASB). Sound familiar? Anxiety multiplies. The word here translated "multiply" means "to be many."

> HE HAS ALREADY MADE OF YOU A BRAND NEW CREATION. THERE IS NO PART OF YOU THAT HE CAN'T RENEW.

When we allow fear to have its way, we often mentally rehearse the worst possible scenarios. Your amygdala is working overtime, providing your brain with the emotions it needs to make your imagination feel so real that you experience emotion as if it were real. Now you have added another emotional memory to your brain, and it cannot distinguish between what actually happened and what you imagined might happen.

In light of this fascinating information about God's ingenious creation we know as our brain, what do we do with it? How does this understanding help us position ourselves for the Holy Spirit to work and to create brand new neural pathways? After all, He has already made of you a brand new creation. There is no part of you that He can't renew. Not one neuron is outside His purview.

How have you noticed mood congruent memory in your bouts with fear and worry?

_____

_____

_____

Have you noticed that when you imagine a negative scenario in detail—really put your heart into it—your brain retrieves the

emotion to go along with your imagined story? Think of a time when this has happened.

_____

_____

_____

_____

AN INTERVENTION

You are beginning to see the orderly process of God's creation. His creation is not chaotic or random, but constructed so that one piece fits into another and His whole creation works together seamlessly, leaving room for Him to make use of His own design to renew, heal, and set us free. His whole creation—every neuron, every molecule, every atom—reveals His nature. "For since the creation of the world God's invisible qualities—his eternal power and divine nature—have been clearly seen, being understood from what has been made" (Romans 1:20). The way your brain works is predictable and orderly, and we can cooperate with the Holy Spirit as He renews our minds by changing our brains.

Now when you find yourself in fear mode, you will understand how you got there. Before, maybe you thought you got to a place of fear and worry because that would be the appropriate response to the situation. The situation produced fear, you reasoned. But God wants to impart to us His own peace, an internal state that external situations cannot disrupt. "Peace I leave with you; _my peace_ I give you. I do not give to you as the world gives. Do not let your hearts be troubled and do not be afraid" (John 14:27, author's emphasis).

He transfuses you with His very own peace. Notice, not a peace _like_ His, but _His_ peace. How can He give you His very own peace? Because He lives in you. Right this minute. In the middle of this situation. Fully present in all His power.

When you find yourself in fear mode, allow the Holy Spirit to stage an intervention. You can recognize what has happened to get you here. You encountered the cue that set off your habit cycle of fear. Maybe you have discovered what some of those cues are, and maybe not. It may not even matter. The cue might be too subtle to recognize. Without thinking or reasoning, you traveled the old, well-worn neural pathway that brought you here. You began to speak—even if by thought—all the worst-case eventualities, and toxic neurochemicals began to flood your brain. Anxious thoughts multiplied—one gave birth to another, and another. Your amygdala has provided all the emotion you need to really get invested in your worry.

Stop. Acknowledge. Interrupt the pattern. That's the first thing. Instead of buying fully into the enemy's lies, start speaking truth. Let me take you back to *Words Can Change Your Brain* for this fascinating scientifically proven reality that lines up perfectly with the Word of God.

> By holding a positive and optimistic thought in your mind, you stimulate frontal lobe activity. This area includes specific language centers that connect directly to the motor cortex responsible for moving you into action. And as our research has shown, the longer you concentrate on positive words, the more you begin to affect other areas of the brain. Functions in the parietal lobe start to change, which changes your perception of yourself and the people you interact with. A positive view of yourself will bias you toward seeing the good

in others, whereas a negative self-image will incline you toward suspicion and doubt. Over time the structure of your thalamus will also change in response to your conscious words, thoughts, and feelings, and we believe that the thalamic changes affect the way in which you perceive reality.

By saying positive, true words—God's Words of hope—dopamine (the feel-good neurotransmitter that helps control the brain's reward center) begins to flow. Your brain begins to change, and your mind is being renewed.

God will teach you and train you in how to speak true and uplifting words to yourself. I wrote the following in my book *The Power of Small.*

> *"The Sovereign Lord has given me an instructed tongue, to know the word that sustains the weary. He wakens me morning by morning, wakens my ear to listen like one being taught."* (Isaiah 50:4)
>
> An instructed tongue. Not a wild untamed tongue, or a go-its-own-way tongue. We can have a trained, disciplined, controlled tongue. He wants you to speak words taught you by the Spirit. (See 1 Corinthians 2:13.) When you speak with an instructed tongue, what kind of power do your words have? They have the power to sustain the weary.
>
> Words generated in my own wisdom can reach only as far as a person's intellect or feelings. Words that are taught by the Spirit reach deep into the person and touch the spirit: "Deep calls to deep" (Psalm 42:7). Spirit-generated words can touch the spirit because

they are "expressing spiritual truths in spiritual words" (1 Corinthians 2:13). These words are spiritual words because they were born of the Spirit. Everything that is born of the Spirit is spirit.

How do you learn the words that lift up the weary? "He wakens me morning by morning, wakens my ear to listen like one being taught" (Isaiah 50:4). You learn by listening, listening carefully, attentively, like a student soaking up every word his mentor speaks. Respond to the Father's initiative. He wakens you morning after morning and unstops your spiritual ears.

The Father wants to speak His healing, encouraging, strengthening, eternal, life-giving words through your mouth. He wants to instruct your tongue. When He sends His word out through you, He has already given that word an assignment. The astonishing power of His Word will accomplish what He desires and purposes. (Read Isaiah 55:10–11.)

As you live moment by moment in His power and presence, He will speak His present-tense word through you. "The lips of the righteous nourish many" (Proverbs 10:21). You will speak what you have heard from the Father.

When I wrote this, I was focused on the words we speak to others, but the words we speak to ourselves have the same effect. Words can tear down or words can build up. The words we learn from the Lord uplift and encourage.

THE TONGUE IS A SMALL PART OF THE BODY, BUT IT MAKES GREAT BOASTS. CONSIDER WHAT A GREAT FOREST IS SET ON FIRE BY A SMALL SPARK. THE TONGUE ALSO IS A FIRE, A WORLD OF EVIL AMONG THE

PARTS OF THE BODY. IT CORRUPTS THE WHOLE BODY, SETS THE WHOLE COURSE OF ONE'S LIFE ON FIRE, AND IS ITSELF SET ON FIRE BY HELL.
—JAMES 3:5–6

What are some negative, fearful things you have said to yourself and expected for your future? Write some familiar phrases and words that you recognize from your own thoughts.

Now, cross through each of them with a big, black marker (if you have one) so your paper looks like it has been redacted by the government. Beside each lie, write truth. As you go, ask the Lord to give you an instructed tongue to speak only truth to yourself.

Next, plan your intervention. You know your personality. What works for you to open yourself to the Spirit's work to interrupt the fear habit cycle? Read Scripture? Sing praise songs? Write in your journal? Make a plan. If you are an extrovert, you might want to get together with someone else and speak words with an instructed tongue. If you are an introvert, you might find more meaning in solitude.

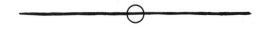

Not only do we need to have an intervention when we find ourselves in fear mode but also we need to flood our brains continually with the truth of God's Word and let His Word form neural connections. God tells us to create those neural pathways so that they lead us to reality and truth. "Set your minds on things above, not on earthly things" (Colossians 3:2).

May I suggest that you start journaling, or saving in your smartphone, tablet, or device, Scriptures God uses to speak hope and healing to you? In the last week of this study, you will find Scriptures to remind you of God's truths that flush out Satan's lies. You know that you can't decide not to think about something. Rather, you have to change the direction of your thoughts to think about something else. You can't simply choose not think about the lie. You have to ponder, meditate on, and talk about the truth.

> YOU CAN'T SIMPLY CHOOSE NOT THINK ABOUT THE LIE. YOU HAVE TO PONDER, MEDITATE ON, AND TALK ABOUT THE TRUTH.

One last thought. Does this mean you shouldn't share your fears or sorrows or discouragements? No. You need to be able to express your struggle. Just don't park there. When you are expressing your struggle, know that you are just passing through. Express it as you need to and feel free to be brutally honest, but have another destination in mind. Don't rehearse the negative aspect so often that you form a new neural pathway to discouragement or fear.

THE PROMISE OF PRAYER

The promise of prayer is a transformed heart. Through the ongoing discipline of prayer, we are brought into direct and intimate contact with the Father's heart. As we continually behold His glory, we are changed into His image. Our lives begin to reflect Him; our desires begin to reflect His desires. As He has constant access to us, He realigns our vision, recreates our desires, reproduces His heart. Powerful, earth-changing prayer begins in the heart of God and flows through the hearts of His people. The promise of prayer is a heart that matches His.

—*Live a Praying Life*®

DAY ONE
RECOGNIZING THE TRUTH

THIS WEEK WE LOOK AT THE PROMISE OF PRAYER IN RELATION TO LIVING WITHOUT FEAR. The promise of prayer is not a secret formula that will make God carry out your wishes and act on your ideas. The promise of prayer is a heart and mind so conformed to His that faith takes the place of fear. Instead of living with fear as our default position, faith becomes our default position. Peace reigns. Joy flows. This week we will discover strategies to cooperate with the Holy Spirit as He moves in us to renew our minds.

WHERE DOES FEAR COME FROM?

We've already recognized that fear is a weapon that comes from Satan, whose tactic is to kill, steal, and destroy. In Scripture, this is directly in contrast to Jesus' intention.

> THE THIEF COMES ONLY TO STEAL AND KILL AND DESTROY; I HAVE COME THAT THEY MAY HAVE LIFE, AND HAVE IT TO THE FULL. —JOHN 10:10

These two emphatic statements contradict each other. The thief—Satan—comes "only to steal and kill and destroy." No other goal. No other agenda. He is set on his purpose. He wants to steal, kill, and destroy what Jesus wants to give. He wants to steal abundant life. Everything he does, or arranges, has his mission in mind. Just what is his mission? His tactics are to steal, kill, and destroy, but his mission is to become like God. That was his stated intention from the beginning.

YOU SAID IN YOUR HEART, "I WILL ASCEND TO THE HEAVENS; I WILL RAISE MY THRONE ABOVE THE STARS OF GOD; I WILL SIT ENTHRONED ON THE MOUNT OF ASSEMBLY, ON THE UTMOST HEIGHTS OF MOUNT ZAPHON. I WILL ASCEND ABOVE THE TOPS OF THE CLOUDS; I WILL MAKE MYSELF LIKE THE MOST HIGH." —ISAIAH 14:13–14

Think about how introducing fear and worry into your thoughts is Satan's attempt to dethrone God in your life. As in the beginning with Eve, he hints to you that God might not be all He claims to be. Isn't that the essence of fear? *Don't* hear me saying that when we fear or worry we are worshiping Satan. I'm *not* saying that. But when you look at the big picture, you can see how we can fall prey to his ploys. He's a clever one.

His cleverness compared to God's wisdom is no contest. Not even in the same universe. Paul describes Christ as the one "in whom are hidden *all* the treasures of wisdom and knowledge" (Colossians 2:3, author's emphasis). In 1 Corinthians 1:30, Paul refers to Jesus as our wisdom: "who has become for us wisdom from God." Jesus embodies God's wisdom, and Jesus lives in you. When you encounter the clever tactics of your enemy, he is already outmatched. The arena in which the enemy uses his skills is your mind. But Jesus has you covered. You have the mind of Christ (1 Corinthians 2:16). You have direct and immediate access to His thoughts, His wisdom. He can show you your situation from His viewpoint.

HOW IS GOD TELLING YOUR STORY?

When you and I tell our stories about what is going on in our lives to cause us fear and worry, we tend to tell it as it looks from earth. We lay out the facts, we interpret those facts, and we talk about the facts. Certainly there is nothing wrong with that. But we must realize that when God tells the same story, it sounds very different. In

Week One, Day Four, we looked at the Hebrews' story after Joseph died as it is told from earth's point of view in Exodus 1 and contrasted his story with how it is told from heaven's point of view in Psalm 105. Review that section.

When we tell our stories, we are usually the main actors. When God tells the story, it is all His activity. When we tell our stories, we tell what "happened." When God tells the story, He tells what He arranged and intentionally allowed. He points out the places where He redirected, warned of danger, and held back what might have occurred.

Write out your right-now story as God is telling it. What does He see that you do not?

Now, tell God's version to someone else. Let your brain hear the true words.

As God renews your mind, He teaches you how to see from heaven's point of view and how to navigate each moment in light of reality instead of your limited earthly view. I wrote the following in my book *Live a Praying Life® in Adversity*. See if this illustration helps you more fully grasp what I mean.

> Jesus suggested to Nicodemus that the Spirit is like the wind. Once again, Jesus points to an earth picture to explain a spirit truth. The wind has no substance. You don't know where it comes from or where it's going. You can't grab hold of it and feel its texture. You only know wind because of its effects.
>
> Suppose, then, that a person decides that he does not believe in the wind. Wind, he decides, is the figment of someone's imagination. No one can prove wind. He prefers to stick to things that can be empirically proven. This person will reach some strange conclusions about what is true. For example, this person will conclude that trees lean over all by themselves sometimes or that leaves lying quietly on the ground sometimes jump up and twirl through the air. This person will ascribe power where there is no power. He will not understand that the trees and the leaves are responding to a power that is acting on them.
>
> If a person who does not believe in the wind and a person who believes in and understands the wind look at the same scene, they will see two startlingly different

truths. The first will see trees bending over; the second will see the wind.

The person who learns to observe with spirit eyes will look at earth and see Spirit. This person will understand that everything he sees on the earth is the effect of spirit. This person will know and understand the whole truth, the reality, and will not be limited to time bound, earthbound perceptions and shortsighted vision.

I challenge you to stop looking at the tree bending over and start looking at the wind blowing. "For we live by faith, not by sight" (2 Corinthians 5:7).

So we fix our eyes not on what is seen, but on what is unseen, since what is seen is temporary, but what is unseen is eternal.
—2 Corinthians 4:18

DAY TWO
REWRITING THE SCRIPT

EVERYTHING—EVERY SINGLE THING, NO EXCEPTIONS—THAT
SATAN MEANS FOR EVIL, GOD INTENDS FOR GOOD. As Joseph
declares in Genesis 50:20, "You intended to harm me, but God
intended it for good to accomplish what is now being done, the saving of many lives."

I want you to zero in on the word "intended." You see that God
is not saying, "Since it has happened, I'll find a way to use it for
good." He *intends* it. The *Theological Wordbook of the Old Testament*
explains, "the basic idea of the word is the employment of the mind
in thinking activity. Reference is not so much to 'understanding,'
but to the creating of new ideas." He has actively intended it, and for
your good and the good of those involved.

YOUR GOOD AND HIS GLORY

Let me go off on a little tangent here and insert a parenthetical idea
that we do need to deal with. I can't tell you how many times over
the years I have heard the fear expressed: "I'm afraid God will cause
something terrible to happen so He can use it for His glory."

First, God does not inflict harm. He most often deflects harm.
You will not have trials and challenges and heartaches because you
are a Christ follower. You will have troubles *because* you live in this
fallen world. Every difficulty that will not be optimum for your betterment will be turned away. He has weighed it in the balance and
has determined that the good it will produce far outweighs the pain
it will cause. He carefully guards and watches over you and those

you love. Nothing comes to you as punishment because the full force of your punishment was enacted on Jesus. Nothing comes to you because God was distracted or not powerful enough to stop it.

Second, God's glory and your good are not mutually exclusive. He doesn't just mean "for your own good" like an evil stepmother in the movies might mean. He is not growling it, and saying, "There! Take that! That'll teach ya." Your good—your benefit, your profit, your betterment—is His glory. When you are living in the abundant, overflowing joy and peace He wants to impart, then He is glorified. People often point to the way a believer walks through heartache and shows the power of God in his or her life as the way God gets glory. And that is true. But it is not the end goal. After you have walked through and processed your pain, you will come out the other side and have joy again. You will have new dimensions of joy and peace that add immeasurably to your life and that could not have come to you any other way.

> AFTER YOU HAVE WALKED THROUGH AND PROCESSED YOUR PAIN, YOU WILL COME OUT THE OTHER SIDE AND HAVE JOY AGAIN.

> FOR HE DOES NOT WILLINGLY BRING AFFLICTION OR GRIEF TO ANYONE.
> —LAMENTATIONS 3:33

> MAY THOSE WHO DELIGHT IN MY VINDICATION SHOUT FOR JOY AND GLADNESS; MAY THEY ALWAYS SAY, "THE LORD BE EXALTED, *WHO DELIGHTS IN THE WELL-BEING OF HIS SERVANT.*"
> —PSALM 35:27, AUTHOR'S EMPHASIS

John Piper has said, "God is most glorified in us when we are most satisfied in him."

A PLATFORM FOR HIS POWER

The situation causing you fear or anxiety right now is an opening for God to show Himself strong on your behalf, and He delights to do so. He's looking for opportunities. "For the eyes of the LORD range throughout the earth to strengthen those whose hearts are fully committed to him" (2 Chronicles 16:9). He is not aloof from your struggle or inured to your pain. He is eagerly waiting for you to turn to Him so He can do for you what you cannot do for yourself.

Let's allow your particular fears and worries to be the catalyst to the deeper work He wants to do in you. It will be work that sets you free to live in His abundance because that is what He came to accomplish. That's what He does.

Fear and worry can be signposts that identify areas of weakness in your life. I don't mean character flaws. I mean places in your soul and personality that have been weakened by wounds inflicted, or experiences that have left their mark. God wants to heal those and make you whole. Let your fear be God's great big flashing sign that says, "Here is where I want to work. Right here."

Drill down into that fear and look at it inside out. You have already stated your fear. "I'm afraid that (what will happen?)." So, what if that did happen? What if the worst-case scenario materialized? Let's talk about that for a minute.

It's misguided, at best, for someone to tell you that you don't need to fear because if you have faith nothing fearful will ever happen. You can't base your fearless living on that assumption. Your fearless life is going to be grounded in who God is and will have nothing to do with the ebb and flow of circumstances.

You remember Shadrach, Meshach, and Abednego from the story of Daniel. They were young men in captivity, and Satan engineered a situation he thought would do in their faith and, barring that, would do them in. The king had been persuaded to establish a law that all citizens must worship his gods and bow down to his golden images. The three young men refused, so they were to receive the punishment—to be thrown into a fiery furnace. The fire had been turned up sevenfold just for them. Here is their assessment of the situation:

> IF WE ARE THROWN INTO THE BLAZING FURNACE, THE GOD WE SERVE IS ABLE TO DELIVER US FROM IT, AND HE WILL DELIVER US FROM YOUR MAJESTY'S HAND. *BUT EVEN IF HE DOES NOT*, WE WANT YOU TO KNOW, YOUR MAJESTY, THAT WE WILL NOT SERVE YOUR GODS OR WORSHIP THE IMAGE OF GOLD YOU HAVE SET UP.
> —DANIEL 3:17–18, AUTHOR'S EMPHASIS

First item of faith: He can deliver me from this situation. Second item of faith: He will deliver me from the hand of my enemy. Third item of faith: Even if He does not take me out of the situation, He will deliver me from the enemy's plan to use it against me, He will still be God, He will still be good, and I will still be fine.

CHANGE YOUR FEAR SCRIPT

If everything Satan means for harm, God intends for your good, then that applies to fear. Satan makes use of fear in an effort to cripple you, but God can use it to enrich and strengthen you. Let's look at how your fear and worry can be transformed into instruments of healing.

Maybe you find fear and anxiety ruling your emotions. Perhaps you have seen relationship after relationship poisoned by your need to control because you fear losing control. Maybe you sense a barrier between you and others erected by your sense of inadequacy because you fear being exposed. We are all riddled with soul wounds, and if those wounds are left to fester, their noxious impact oozes into our personalities, our relationships, our emotions, and our thought patterns. Whatever it is that holds you back and diminishes your life, I want to tell you that God desires to set you free.

Your first hint at the areas of your soul that have been weakened by life's hurts, experiences, and wounding words from others is where your fears and worries gravitate.

———————————

As you have identified your fears, have you noticed that your fears tend to cluster around a certain topic? For example, do your fears seem to be about physical danger? Or financial loss? Or what might happen to others, such as your children or spouse, that would be out of your control? Reflect on where you fears fall, and ask the Holy Spirit if He has anything to reveal to you. If it doesn't come together for you, don't worry about it. (Pun intended!)

Your fears can give you a clue as to the places in your soul where wounds fester. They are your symptoms. When you have a physical ailment, you come to a doctor because of symptoms, and that is how diagnosis begins. You can rejoice because you recognize that God brings illness to your attention through symptoms so He can heal you and free you. He does not bring this to your attention so He can condemn you. As you begin to put these pieces together, sense His tenderness for you. Think of a physician pressing on some part of your anatomy and asking, "Does it hurt there?" Getting a sense of where to focus the healing. In God's case, the information is not for Him because He knows it. It is for you.

The healing God pours out in you will go deep. It will soak into your soul and saturate your mind. In the Book of Hebrews we read:

> FOR THE WORD OF GOD IS ALIVE AND ACTIVE. SHARPER THAN ANY DOUBLE-EDGED SWORD, IT PENETRATES EVEN TO DIVIDING SOUL AND SPIRIT, JOINTS AND MARROW; IT JUDGES THE THOUGHTS AND ATTITUDES OF THE HEART. NOTHING IN ALL CREATION IS HIDDEN FROM GOD'S SIGHT. EVERYTHING IS UNCOVERED AND LAID BARE BEFORE THE EYES OF HIM TO WHOM WE MUST GIVE ACCOUNT. —HEBREWS 4:12–13

When written, this might have called to mind for the Jewish audience the role of the priest in examining animals to determine their fitness as sacrifices, since the sacrifice had to be pure, spotless, and without blemish. The priest would examine the skin, then the muscle layer, then the organs, and finally the bones, each layer laid open by the priest's double-edged knife as he prepared the animal to be offered. As the priest cut open the sacrificial animal, he was required to wash the internal organs, making it clean within. (For example, see Leviticus 1:6–9.) The law for the Passover lamb required that it be kept in the home and observed for four days (Exodus 12:3–6), looking for any imperfections. Do you see how thorough the examination was?

You, my friend, are not being examined to see if you are presentable. Your sacrifice—the precious Lamb of God—has already been examined, and no fault or blemish has been found in Him. But the

Word of God is penetrating with its life and energy into the marrow of your soul to bring healing at the deepest levels—even finding and healing the festering memories of which you have no conscious recollection that are bringing fear into your life right now.

David Seamands, in his book *Redeeming the Past*, explains:

> Many of us have hurtful memories that we try to push out of our minds. Such memories cannot be healed by the mere passage of time any more than an infected wound could be. The infection turns inward and actually worsens because it spreads to other areas, affecting and infecting them. So it is with certain painful experiences, especially those that happened during the important years of early childhood and teenage development.

Can you identify past experiences or reasons why your fears might cluster around a certain topic?

As we explore how God wants to set us free to live without fear, we'll focus our attention more on the Healer than on our hurts. Our hurtful memories and experiences will be the platform for God's power and the context for His healing work. We will examine how He can heal memories that feed current fears and how He can teach us to walk in wholeness.

DAY THREE
EMBRACING THE WEAKNESS

INSTEAD OF FEARING OUR FEARS AND WORRYING ABOUT OUR WORRIES, WE ARE GOING TO EMBRACE THEM AS WEAKNESSES IN WHICH GOD IS ABOUT TO SHOW US HIS STRENGTH.

> BUT HE SAID TO ME, "MY GRACE IS SUFFICIENT FOR YOU, FOR MY POWER IS MADE PERFECT IN WEAKNESS." THEREFORE I WILL BOAST ALL THE MORE GLADLY ABOUT MY WEAKNESSES, SO THAT CHRIST'S POWER MAY REST ON ME. THAT IS WHY, FOR CHRIST'S SAKE, I DELIGHT IN WEAKNESSES, IN INSULTS, IN HARDSHIPS, IN PERSECUTIONS, IN DIFFICULTIES. FOR WHEN I AM WEAK, THEN I AM STRONG.
> —2 CORINTHIANS 12:9–10

Instead of seeing fear as a barrier, see it as a starting point. I'm going to let my friend Rachel Holley tell her experience with changing her fear script.

A gradual result of fear taking over was the way life became smaller; contact with others became less frequent, friendships faded away, life became unsatisfying, the door stayed locked, the blinds stayed down, work fell by the wayside.

I remember when I noticed that I had a small life. Every day had become empty, the phone stopped ringing, and I could go days without seeing anyone but store clerks or talking to anyone but bill collectors. I wasn't even trying to reach out anymore; I made no effort to guiltily go to lunch with someone. I knew I could fall off the face of the earth and not that many people would know.

The insidious—or is it the redemptive?—power of fear is found here, in my realization that due to my response to fear, my life had become completely different. The trajectory I'd been on radically reversed itself and, because of my relationship to fear, I was traveling in another direction as another person. All I'd worked for, dreamed of, trained for, and sweated blood for had been changed, seemingly without me having the strength to do anything except be swept along.

We see fear as a negative influence, something we need to learn to manage or medicate; we may go so far as to relive the cause of the fear over and over with a therapist. We see fear as a survival tool, something that teaches us to fight or flee when faced with something threatening (or perceived as such).

I've come to believe fear has had a completely different role in my life, that while we often view fear in a negative light, that view is also the result of fear, fear of what will happen if we give in to fear and instead enhance our ability to practice faith and turn to God.

Fear is a reaction to something we perceive as threatening, or fear can be a reaction to an event or life situation that is seen as a change or as an upheaval.

Fear is such a strong force, in our own minds, it's nearly impossible to fight, or fear is such a strong motivator, it may be our best tool in developing faith.

Fear gives us strong messages we interpret as prophetic of our failure at anything we try to do to, or fear's strong messages point us in the exact direction we need to go to increase rather than decrease the size of our lives.

Fear stops us in our tracks, or fear gives us explicit directions for the next leg of our journey.

How can fear be a tool for growth rather than a way we are crippled in our relationship with God and others? I noticed in looking at my own journey, one seemingly stopped by my fears, that the fear I'd lived with had led me to do the very things I was, in fact, most afraid of. For instance, those primal fears at the root of all fears, fear of being alone, fear of being jobless, fear of having no money, fear of having no family support, no plan, no success, fear of being a failure. All the worst-case scenarios had in fact, played themselves out, and it was my reaction to my own fear, the isolating, withdrawing, the shrinking of my world, that led that to happen. My fear of all those eventualities led me right into the small life that contained all those realities.

Through life inside of this fear, I found not the horrors I imagined when I imagined being alone or broke or lost, I found in every circumstance God took care of those things I turned over to Him. I wasn't alone, I wasn't broke or hungry, I wasn't forgotten. My fear pointed me in the new direction, the next leg of the journey, that allowed me to see my life in big picture terms.

So, while the reality of my outside circumstance didn't change immediately (that would come later), my perception of fear changed; it became less an impediment and more a gift, a lens through which God allowed me to see Him.

HELP IN TIME OF NEED

As Rachel's story emphasizes, those very things we fear turn out not to be as fearful in reality as they are in imagination. Because God.

God does not offer grace for what we imagine, but for what is so. "Let us then approach God's throne of grace with confidence, so that we may receive mercy and find grace to help us *in our time of need*" (Hebrews 4:16, author's emphasis). Let me tell you a big lesson in grace that I learned in time of my need.

Life can change in the time it takes for a doctor to finish a sentence. As short an interlude as is required for breath between words, and the sentence you thought would finish with hope, instead ends with "no cure, no treatment." I sat with my husband and heard those words. Where panic should have been the reaction, instead we both felt a blanket of peace descend and cover us.

Years earlier, we felt the Lord leading us to a praying life, rather than have a prayer life—learning to live prayer as a relationship rather than to say prayers as an activity. This led to The Praying Life Foundation. My husband Wayne was at my side, cheering me on, shouldering the burdens, and sharing the joys. He was a fellow-learner, sounding board, advisor, and protector. In the very early years of the ministry, he was my biggest cheerleader. When I was tempted to sit back and let opportunities go by, he prodded me forward. He was always willing to take on the extra work that fell to him while I made deadlines and traveled to speak. He didn't think of it as a burden, since it just meant taking care of our three young sons—his favorite thing to do.

At a certain point when The Praying Life Foundation seemed ready to take a big step forward—to take it would mean much pressure on the family—Wayne decided to take a huge leap of faith and leave his secular career to become the full-time manager and president of the ministry. He put all his expertise, experience, and his relational skills to work running The Praying Life Foundation. No paycheck. No company car. No company trips. Just three little boys and a wife he believed in.

We grew the ministry from a corner of our dining room to a full-time ministry with office employees and volunteers. Side by side, we prayed together through every decision, every opportunity, and every redirection along the way. Even when, in his last years, he went back to a full-time job in a ministry area he loved, he still was entirely involved in everything about The Praying Life Foundation.

In October of 2005, thinking we were finally about to get an answer for the dizziness that had been diagnosed as an inner ear infection, we instead received the news that Wayne had an advanced case of aggressive brain cancer for which there was essentially no hope of cure. We kept a blog during his illness so that colleagues and friends could stay informed. When I added an entry, usually it was more bad news. He would always say, "But tell them it is well with my soul."

He passed away two months after his diagnosis.

When the fog lifted, I began to realize that I was a *widow*, of all things! I could not imagine continuing in the ministry that had always been ours, never just me. The thought of taking on a new project or coming up with a fresh thought seemed impossible. I couldn't say a whole sentence without breaking into sobs. The first year was excruciating, unless I was speaking, and there I felt a special strength come over me. I didn't leave my house for minor things because I never knew what memory might ambush me and send me into a tailspin in public. I would explain to people, "A widow lives in

> I FIND THAT THE GREAT WOUND INFLICTED ON MY HEART HAS MADE ME DESPERATELY DEPENDENT ON GOD IN WAYS I HAD NEVER KNOWN BEFORE.

my body, and I don't know her. I don't know how she'll act. I don't know what to expect from her. I can't let her out in public."

The next Christmas, all of my sons came home. We prepared to attend Christmas Eve services, one of Wayne's favorite things, and I gathered myself emotionally. My sons were not used to having a mom who cried all the time, and they hovered around me and kept asking, "Are you OK, Mom?"

It hit me. *I'm fragile.* I've never been fragile before.

I taught for years about letting the pain of life's crucifixion moments result in resurrection experiences. In the midst of my own pain, I wondered if I should have added: "Except if your husband dies unexpectedly."

I wondered what might have happened if I took my own teaching and embraced the pain. Would it lead to life? What did Jesus have for me in the midst of that pain?

I find that the great wound inflicted on my heart has made me desperately dependent on God in ways I had never known before. I experienced a level of comfort that can't be explained and can only be experienced.

The widow and I have integrated. I'm not fragile anymore, but I am patient with others who are fragile. I think it is easier to tell people that we can avoid suffering and be protected from all pain than it is to tell people that pain is unavoidable and should be embraced for the work it will do in our lives.

I wrote these words long ago in my book *He Restores My Soul*, and they have never been more profoundly proven than in that moment of my life:

> Pride, or our mistaken sense that you need to present a perfect front to those in our care, causes us to think of our wounds and our scars as something to hide; something ugly; something demeaning; something that lessens our value. But look at Jesus. Look at what Jesus thought of His wounds: "Here, Thomas. Look at My wounds. Touch My scars. These are the proof of My resurrection. I bear the marks of death, but I am alive!" Jesus knew His wounds were beautiful.

> At the places where I am broken, the power of Christ is authenticated in me for others. Where I have submitted to the crucifixion, the power of the resurrection is put on display. I can say, "Look at my wounds. Touch my scars. I have death-wounds, but I am alive." I can wear my wounds without shame. They tell a resurrection story.

If what you fear happens, everything is there for you. In your time of need, you will be surprised by mercy, grace, and help.

How much of your worry and fear is about imagining what might be or what could happen? Is the thing you fear really the most likely possibility?

_____

_____

_____

Can you identify ways that fear or worry have limited your life? Have you passed that limiting fear on to others?

_____

_____

_____

_____

FRUITLESS FEAR

Most of what we fear will never happen. We will waste emotional and mental energy on something that will never touch us. But, even if it does, worrying about it and fearing it in advance will not stop it. We don't have tomorrow's strength today.

I have a fear of mice. I mean a _fear_ fear. It might be my most obsessive fear. I have gadgets in every room of my house that promise to keep mice away. My little gadgets emit staccato sounds all the time, and I'm so used to them that I don't even hear them. But when I have guests, they always ask about the sounds. I have to unplug all my gadgets, or the sounds meant to rid me of mice might, instead, rid me of guests.

I have never had a mouse in my house. If I did, if I reasonably compared my strength to a mouse's strength, I think I'd win. There is nothing fearsome about a mouse, and I know that. That does not diminish my fear.

One morning I reached under my kitchen sink to get something, and in a far back dark corner, I spied a dead mouse. Fear took over. In tears, I called my sister to come over and get it, but she could not get there until the evening. I had made coffee before the mouse sighting, but I couldn't go into my kitchen to get any. I had to go out for food because I couldn't go in my kitchen to get my meals. I spent

125

my day imagining that I heard mice everywhere. My fear consumed all of my mental energy for the day.

When my sister arrived that evening, she put a plastic grocery bag on her hand, opened my cabinet door, and said, "Where is it? I don't see it." You can imagine all the scenarios that sprung to mind. I looked in, saw it, and said, "There! Right there!" She looked at me and said, "That's a sponge."

That is how our fear works. It steals our energy. Your brain takes energy to run all its functions. Your brain uses as much as 25 percent of your body's daily energy expenditure. When your brain is hosting fear, that is where your energy goes. Fear is an energy hog. You don't notice things that need your attention. Your life is restricted by your fear. All that energy put into something that never happens, or if it does happen will not be as monumental as your imagination of it.

Living in fear and worry makes no sense. We need some practical tools and strategies for how to interrupt the fear habit loop, and we will get to that. First, let's continue to build a good understanding of fear so we can be informed and adept at combating it.

DAY FOUR
UNCOVERING THE HIDDEN FEARS

"Keep your heart with all diligence, for out of it is the wellspring of life" (Proverbs 4:23 WEB). Here, the Hebrew word translated *heart* could accurately be rendered "mind." It is the center of thought, reasoning, and emotion. Your mind is the wellspring of life. A wellspring is "a source of continual or abundant supply."

All of your reactions, responses, and emotions flow from your heart and mind. If the source, the wellspring, is contaminated, everything that flows from it will be, too. As Jesus said, "A good man brings good things out of the good stored up in him, and an evil man brings evil things out of the evil stored up in him" (Matthew 12:35).

GUARD YOUR WELLSPRING

In my book, *When You Hurt and When He Heals*, I discuss how our minds receive and input information:

> Your mind organizes information and experiences and assigns meaning to them. It files them for you and gives them labels. It also compares new input and experiences to existing files and cross-references them so that old thoughts, feelings, beliefs, and experiences help define new ones. In this way, new experiences are automatically linked to old ones.

Because of the way your mind works, something that enters your experience today will very likely evoke emotions and fears

128

associated with experiences from the past. This is so ingrained that the process goes unnoticed. It feels to you like a response to the present moment, but it is really a cumulative response from cross-referenced experiences throughout your life. If, for example, early in your life you had numerous experiences that your mind labeled "rejection," those files are filled with self-loathing. The meaning your mind assigned was, "I'm unlovable. I'm not good enough. I'm incompetent." Later, as new files were added, you began to have files labeled "anger," "defensiveness," "need to prove my worth," "need to be right." You fear rejection, and that fear drives many of your interactions and responses.

All these files are linked and cross-referenced. Every new experience and interaction is defined by the beliefs already on file. So you interpret most experiences as rejection, either overt or subtle. That activates the self-loathing file, which activates the defensiveness file, which activates the anger file, which activates the need to be right file. And they are all filed under the heading "fear." You can't open one file without all linked files opening with it.

A friend of mine grew up in squalid poverty. Her early days were filled with shame and embarrassment. She was looked down on and scorned. Today she is a beautiful and accomplished woman. She was, however, extremely defensive when anyone tried to correct her or even make a suggestion to her. She read criticism into many comments that were not even slightly critical. She felt compelled to cover over any small mistake she might make by lying about it. She was crippled by fear of how others might perceive her. Her reactions seemed justified to her.

Gradually she realized she was living in the fear that if anyone knew the "real her," they would look down on and reject her. She feared that any slipping of her façade would show that little, barefoot, dirty girl she once was. As she healed, she became aware of her reactions: "When I felt all those defensive and shame files opening, I'd step back from the moment mentally and spiritually. I asked the Spirit to show me truth. I intentionally lined my reactions up with truth. After years of practice, the truth is now my truth."

The power of the living God can refile and redefine your past experiences and bring healing to memories that have colored your present experiences. He will not change the past, but He will allow you to see the past through His eyes. You can revisit those old, hurtful experiences, and, with the Holy Spirit as your loving guide, you can "extract the precious from the worthless" (Jeremiah 15:19 NASB). For example, you can see the things that have added wisdom or compassion or dependence on God that could have come in no other way. You can see the ways that God was present, protecting you from the full force of your experience. In that old memory, you might also recognize a lie that you embraced about yourself or about God. When you identify those lies that have worked themselves into the fabric of your life and have poisoned your wellspring, you then have the freedom to deliberately and willfully reject them. You can start the process of replacing them with the truth that sets you free.

> HE WILL NOT CHANGE THE PAST, BUT HE WILL ALLOW YOU TO SEE THE PAST THROUGH HIS EYES.

If we can be brutally and fearlessly honest with ourselves, many of our fears are linked, at least in part, to the fear of what others will think. If your fears cluster around finances—job loss, collapsing economy, going broke—isn't part of your fear about what others will think? If your fears cluster around your children—rebelling, making poor decisions, getting trapped in drugs—isn't part of your fear about what others will think?

What if we could just confess that and let Jesus take it over for us? Doesn't that element just add unnecessary worry? Again, don't start condemning yourself if this is hitting home with you. Instead, embrace it as a moment when you are going to shake off something that has been paralyzing you or slowing your progress without you even realizing it was there. "Fear of man will prove to be a snare, but whoever trusts in the LORD is kept safe" (Proverbs 29:25).

————————

Do you recognize some files in your mind that are activating fear or worry in you right now?

_____

_____

_____

Can you think back on experiences that are coloring your present perceptions and reframe them as positive instead of negative?

_____

_____

_____

As you analyze your fears, do you recognize in any of them an element of the fear of what others will think? I know that fears are complex and multifaceted, but is some part of your fear linked to your reputation?

FEAR OF MAN

Fear of man can hold you back from fully embracing Jesus.

> YET AT THE SAME TIME MANY EVEN AMONG THE LEADERS BELIEVED IN HIM. BUT BECAUSE OF THE PHARISEES THEY WOULD NOT OPENLY ACKNOWLEDGE THEIR FAITH FOR FEAR THEY WOULD BE PUT OUT OF THE SYNAGOGUE; FOR THEY LOVED HUMAN PRAISE MORE THAN PRAISE FROM GOD. —JOHN 12:42–43

That's what it boils down to. We love human praise more than praise from God. Ouch! That's a hard thing to recognize about yourself, but it will be the beginning of freedom from many of your fears. Recognizing this reality can help you identify what you have been trying to get from others that can really only come from God.

When you recognize this aspect of your fear, now that it is out in the open and seen clearly, reject it. Turn your heart toward Jesus. Embrace the reality that the very thing you desire to get from other people, Jesus is ready to flood you with right now. Realize that it is another area of life that you can't control, and no amount of effort will assure you that other people will ever give you what you need. Turn that need to Him. Ask Him to point out to you when fear of others' opinions is playing a part in your life and emotions. "Test me, LORD, and try me, examine my heart and my mind; for I have always been mindful of your unfailing love and have lived in reliance on your faithfulness" (Psalm 26:2–3).

HIDDEN THINGS

"He reveals deep and hidden things; he knows what lies in darkness, and light dwells with him" (Daniel 2:22). Many of the experiences that color your present may not be things that you consciously recall. Several things can account for this. Let's examine them one by one.

132

Memories of events throughout your life are stored in deep storage in your brain. Impressions, experiences, and emotions are banked in your subconscious mind. These stored memories and impressions actively shape your perceptions in the present. Every experience you have today will be filtered through a paradigm that your mind has constructed over your lifetime. You will respond to today in light of all your yesterdays, dating back to impressions made even in the womb.

Recent research strongly suggests that babies in the womb respond to sounds and emotions and retain memories. As a baby, you are unaware of many of the occurrences around you, least of all those that dictate your reactions and perceptions today. Some of these impressions became embedded in your emotional memory from the time when the universe of your mind consisted only of sensation and imagery. You had no logic or ability to evaluate or reason. Yet they are part of you forever.

The part of your brain that activates factual memory—memory of events, who people are, etc.—is called the hippocampus. The part that activates emotional memory—the stored emotion from an event—is called the amygdala, as we have already seen. The hippocampus is not fully developed before the age of three, but the amygdala is present from the time you are a fetus. Therefore, your brain may have stored an emotional memory, but your brain has no factual memory to go with it. Many of your earliest memories are recorded only as impressions and emotions.

You don't consciously remember the event. This gives the impressions more power, because to you it's something you "just know." It doesn't seem to have come from a skewed view of an event because you don't remember the event. Only the emotion lives in your mind. But the Father, who knit you together in your mother's womb, knows. You can ask Him to bring healing into your earliest, precognitive memories. You can invite Him into your emotional memory to do a deep work that He alone can do. He can remove the toxins from those memories and leave them powerless. You don't have to consciously remember an event to ask the Spirit, who searches the deep and hidden things, to heal.

DEEP STORAGE

Your unawareness of experiences that color your present-day perceptions and reactions might also be caused by the conscious mind's ability to suppress painful memories. Sometimes events or circumstances are too much for you to deal with at the time, so as a protective defense, your mind sets the memories aside. Perhaps you can cope with it better later, or perhaps your subconscious will try to push it down forever. When a memory pathway goes unused for a period of time, your brain prunes it and puts it into deep storage.

Stored memories are not forgotten. They are on file in your subconscious mind. Because they are not recognized, they are able to wreak havoc in your emotions undetected. The memories actually surface through your emotional responses such as fear, anxiety, anger, worry, insecurity, jealousy, and the like. However, because you don't consciously recognize them, you're not aware of what they are doing.

These memories need not be of monumentally traumatic events. They can be things that were just difficult for you to process at that point of your development. In most cases, these buried memories are not seismic events. When they happened, they seemed hurtful or traumatic at the moment. Their power lies in how you felt them or interpreted them in that moment.

The processes in your brain that create memory are fascinating. Your brain divides its work into highly specialized functions. One area analyzes and files smell, another area handles visual input, yet another deals with auditory input, and so on. One area deals with factual information and another with emotion.

Within these specialized areas, the breakdown is even more detailed. For example, in the occipital lobe, where visual information is translated and stored, a certain area deals with color, another with shape, still another with movement. Then there's size and depth. And the list goes on.

When your brain encodes a memory, neurons from all these different areas create a bond, a pathway to each other. The physical structure of your brain actually changes and is different than it was before you stored that memory. Therefore, a cue that activates one aspect of a given memory can then automatically activate the whole memory. I just find that fascinating. The more you relive a given event, dwelling on it and focusing on all the emotions, the stronger the neural connections—the memory pathways—become.

Your amygdala stores the emotion of the memory. According to *Memory: From Mind to Molecules* by Larry R. Squire and Eric R. Kandel, emotional memory takes precedence over any other kind of memory.

When something cues a memory that is in deep storage and the neural pathway that links all the pieces of that memory starts firing, your brain gives precedence to the emotion of the memory. It comes first and it stays longest. We are adept at quickly pushing that memory back down into storage, but the emotion has surfaced and will have to find a place to be expressed. So, fear, anger born of fear, resentment, or defensiveness with fear at its base—emotions are triggered, and we find ourselves caught up in fear with no clear understanding of what triggered it.

What to do with all this biological information? Let it inform your moments. When you are struggling with fear and worry, don't just believe what your fear is telling you. Your fear is telling you that the emotion you feel is all caused by what is happening right now. Your fear will tell you that you need to fear. Your fear will tell you that it is real and that you have good reason to fear. But you know that fear never has to be your response to any situation because of who God is.

Exchange fear's lies for God's truth. Interrupt the pattern. Insert God's Word where fear used to have the only voice.

THEREFORE WE WILL NOT FEAR, THOUGH THE EARTH GIVE WAY AND THE MOUNTAINS FALL INTO THE HEART OF THE SEA. —PSALM 46:2

DAY FIVE
EMBRACING THE PRESENCE

WE'VE TACKLED A LOT OF TECHNICAL INFORMATION THIS WEEK. I think when you develop an understanding of something, you are better able to make use of it for positive purposes. God designed your brain so that it would be useful to Him and also so that it would be useful to you.

Today, let's change course. Let's just talk about how fear can work for you and move you forward. We talked earlier about the fact that fear can identify weak places, places where God can demonstrate strength. Fear and worry can be the open door to God's power to show you just how amazing He is.

Satan designed fear so that it would be in direct opposition to what God wants for your life. Whatever fear brings into your life or relationships, God wants to produce just the opposite. What does Scripture teach us about God that will make our fears flee?

GOD IS IN THE DETAILS

THE LOT IS CAST INTO THE LAP, BUT ITS EVERY DECISION IS FROM THE LORD. —PROVERBS 16:33

God is in the details. One of the most important truths God wove into His Word is that He engineers even the smallest detail in order to establish His divine purpose in every situation. Happenings that seem random, choices and decisions that seem spontaneous and uncalculated, paths that cross in a seemingly serendipitous way—all are being put in order by the Lord. "The LORD makes firm the steps of the one who delights in him" (Psalm 37:23).

Does anything seem more random than the casting of lots? It seems to be dependent on chance or luck. Yet the Scripture teaches us that even what seems unplanned or uncontrolled is actually ordered by the Lord.

Nothing—not one detail—is random. God, in His Word, points us to His ways. "I meditate on your precepts and consider your ways" (Psalm 119:15). He wants us to consider, learn, and observe His ways and well-worn paths. The way He does things. God tells us to observe and learn His consistent methods of dealing with situations and people. When we know His ways and recognize the underlying consistency in all His doings, we will begin to see the divine will in the center of everything. It is His way to manage the details and to act according to an eternal plan. "LORD, you are my God; I will exalt you and praise your name, for in perfect faithfulness you have done wonderful things, things planned long ago" (Isaiah 25:1). Whatever is happening in your life right now, even though it may seem out of control, even though it may seem as if circumstances are taking on a momentum of their own, God is acting according to a plan that has been in place since the beginning of time. It may look as if the lot has been cast randomly, but remember: the Lord determines how it falls. God shows us His ways through every page of Scripture. He uses everything to work out His own purposes.

> How often we look upon God as our last and feeblest resource! We go to him because we have nowhere else to go. And then we learn that the storms of life have driven us, not upon the rocks, but into the desired haven.
> —*George MacDonald*

CLING

FOR YOU HAVE BEEN MY REFUGE, A STRONG TOWER AGAINST THE FOE. I LONG TO DWELL IN YOUR TENT FOREVER AND TAKE REFUGE IN THE SHELTER OF YOUR WINGS. —PSALM 61:3–4

Under His wings. This is a visual God often uses in His Word to describe His intimate and protective love for us. It calls to mind a scenario in nature with which His people were familiar—the sight of a mother bird gathering her chicks under her wing.

From there, pressed up against the mother, the little chicks gather her warmth and find shelter from both weather and predators. There they have no fear, held safe from any danger.

David uses the same imagery in Psalm 63:7 (NLT): "Because you are my helper, I sing for joy in the shadow of your wings." We find joy in His intimate embrace. We are to live under His wings; we are to make the shadow of His wings our dwelling place. He invites us to a life pressed into Him. David completes this thought with these words: "I cling to you; your strong right hand holds me securely" (Psalm 63:8 NLT). I think the invitation to such intimacy—pressed against His very heart—is rightly met with David's response: "I *cling* to you."

> DO YOU FEEL LIKE YOU ARE ON YOUR OWN? CLING TO JESUS.

I love the word *cling*. Adhere to, stuck like glue, no letting go, pressed in. It makes me think of static cling. Some kind of electrical attraction gets hold of something, and it sticks to you. You can't unstick it. If you try to brush it off, it jumps right back on. It clings.

Cling to Jesus. Is anything troubling you right now? Do you feel vulnerable or exposed or unprotected? Are there circumstances that seem threatening? Do you feel like you are on your own? Cling to

Jesus. Take refuge under His wings. Hear His heart. Let Him warm you and cover you. Stop now and deliberately respond to His invitation: "Come, child. Let me spread My wings over you. Come into the shelter of My presence."

ANTIDOTE TO ANXIETY

> ARE NOT FIVE SPARROWS SOLD FOR TWO PENNIES? YET NOT ONE OF THEM IS FORGOTTEN BY GOD. INDEED, THE VERY HAIRS OF YOUR HEAD ARE ALL NUMBERED. DON'T BE AFRAID; YOU ARE WORTH MORE THAN MANY SPARROWS. —LUKE 12:6–7

Jesus wants to drive home a point. He wants to make sure that we really see what He is promising. He wants to paint a picture in our minds that will stick with us. We don't have to fear anything because God—Creator God, Ruler God, Power-over-Life-and-Death God—values us.

We have great worth to Him. He cherishes us. It's so incongruent that Jesus adds some texture—a way to grab hold of the essence of the promise with a description meant to anchor it in our understanding.

When Jesus spoke these words, He and His audience were outside. Maybe the marketplace was in view, and they could see off in the distance someone purchasing some sparrows, the cheapest and least valued bird. The fare of the poor, for the most part. Imagine Jesus pointing in that direction, framing the scene in His hearers' imaginations. "What is the price of five sparrows—two copper coins?"

It was a teaching method Jesus liked to use—moving from the lesser to the greater. God is fully aware of every single sparrow, Jesus emphasizes. A creature of little value. Cheap. If God watches over every sparrow, then surely He watches over you and me.

We don't have to be afraid of anything, anytime, anywhere. God's protection and provision for us is so microscopic that He knows how many hairs are on our heads. Nothing escapes His notice. Nothing gets past Him. Nothing is hidden from His sight. So, the conclusion we are to reach? Don't be afraid.

PRESENT TO THE PRESENCE

WHY ARE YOU LOOKING AMONG THE DEAD FOR SOMEONE WHO IS ALIVE? HE ISN'T HERE! HE IS RISEN FROM THE DEAD! —LUKE 24:5–6 NLT

We serve a risen, living, present Lord. We don't have to try to find Him among musty laws, stale ceremonies, or stagnant rituals. We don't seek the living among the dead.

The promise of a vibrant and attendant Savior who offers His own power, wisdom, and peace in any given moment is the promise that gathers all other promises into one. He offers Himself. When we have Him, we have everything the Father has to give.

GOD IN ALL HIS FULLNESS WAS PLEASED TO LIVE IN CHRIST. —COLOSSIANS 1:19 NLT

CHRIST, IN WHOM ARE HIDDEN ALL THE TREASURES OF WISDOM AND KNOWLEDGE. —COLOSSIANS 2:2–3

FOR IN CHRIST LIVES ALL THE FULLNESS OF GOD IN A HUMAN BODY. SO YOU ALSO ARE COMPLETE THROUGH YOUR UNION WITH CHRIST, WHO IS THE HEAD OVER EVERY RULER AND AUTHORITY. —COLOSSIANS 2:9–10 NLT

He is so present that He is in you, making Himself available to you and through you. He is living in you—in your world, in your circumstance. Is it possible to encounter any situation for which Jesus is not adequate? Is it possible to have any dilemma for which Jesus does not have wisdom? Is it possible to experience any challenge for which Jesus is not equipped? If you have Jesus—living, right-now Jesus—then you have all you need.

What concerns you right now? What frightens you right now? Hand it over to Jesus, who is closer to you and more available to you than any human being can ever be. Sit quietly and let the reality of His presence settle on you. Take time to be aware. Be present to the Presence.

What truth about God most speaks to you today? What promise or invitation most pulls at your heart and addresses your particular fears and worries?

_____

_____

_____

_____

_____

_____

_____

_____

THE PRACTICE OF PRAYER

The pursuit of any goal requires a narrowed focus. Choosing to live a praying life—a life through which the power of God is free to flow—involves sacrifice. In this, it is no different from any other rock-solid commitment. Whatever you choose to pursue will mean that you sacrifice something else. The key is this: If the goal is sufficiently attractive, the sacrifice required will be irrelevant. In fact, the more focused on your goal you are, the less you will perceive the requirements as "sacrifices."

What you have to give up in order to reach your goal will feel more like being freed of weights. "Let us throw off everything that hinders and the sin that so easily entangles, and let us run with perseverance the race marked out for us" (Hebrews 12:1). What we once considered gain, we now see as loss. What we once counted as treasure, we now know is rubbish.

But whatever was to my profit I now consider loss for the sake of Christ. —Philippians 3:7

—*Live a Praying Life*®

TAKE ACTION: PRAISE

LET'S REVIEW. The battle is in your thoughts. Your brain is where your thoughts are generated and managed. God has designed your brain so that it works for His purposes because it was created for Him. Right now, your brain has many neural pathways that lead to fear and worry. You have the habit of fear. When your brain encounters something or someone or some memory that cues fear, you get caught in the habit loop and land there without intention. Just, there you are.

The key to freedom, as we discussed briefly last week, is to interrupt the pattern. Do this immediately, as soon as you recognize that you are going down that road, or even have gone down that road. Remember, you are taking an action that is constructive and consequential. You are not just trying to feel better in the moment. You are building a new highway.

PLAN OF ACTION

Each day this week, we will implement one action to interrupt the fear pattern. Practice it for a day, then journal your observations and experiences to share with your group.

INTERRUPT THE PATTERN WITH PRAISE AND THANKSGIVING

GIVE THANKS IN ALL CIRCUMSTANCES; FOR THIS IS GOD'S WILL FOR YOU IN CHRIST JESUS. —1 THESSALONIANS 5:18

THROUGH JESUS, THEREFORE, LET US CONTINUALLY OFFER TO GOD A SACRIFICE OF PRAISE—THE FRUIT OF LIPS THAT OPENLY PROFESS HIS NAME. —HEBREWS 13:15

DO NOT BE ANXIOUS ABOUT ANYTHING, BUT IN EVERY SITUATION, BY PRAYER AND PETITION, WITH THANKSGIVING, PRESENT YOUR REQUESTS TO GOD. —PHILIPPIANS 4:6

Even before fear starts, begin praising and thanking God as an inoculation against fear. Certainly, the moment you sense the pattern of the fear habit loop starting—if you recognize a fear cue—override it with praise and thanksgiving. Deliberately move your thoughts from your fear to your Savior.

Thank God for everything you can see of His hand in your fear-inducing situation. Then thank Him because you know that He is working in ways you cannot see. Thank Him for what He is accomplishing through the situation. Then, focus your mind and heart on Him and who He is. Sing or listen to praise music. Talk to someone about how great God is. God instructs us to tell each other about His deeds in our lives. It strengthens your heart and encourages the hearts of others. Read Psalm 22:22; Psalm 26:12; and Psalm 35:28.

Journal your experience. What did you learn? What did you observe?

WHATEVER IS HAPPENING IN YOUR LIFE RIGHT NOW, EVEN THOUGH IT MAY SEEM OUT OF CONTROL, EVEN THOUGH IT MAY SEEM AS IF CIRCUMSTANCES ARE TAKING ON A MOMENTUM OF THEIR OWN, GOD IS ACTING ACCORDING TO A PLAN THAT HAS BEEN IN PLACE SINCE THE BEGINNING OF TIME. IT MAY LOOK AS IF THE LOT HAS BEEN CAST RANDOMLY, BUT REMEMBER: THE LORD DETERMINES HOW IT FALLS. GOD SHOWS US HIS WAYS THROUGH EVERY PAGE OF SCRIPTURE. HE USES EVERYTHING TO WORK OUT HIS OWN PURPOSES.

TAKE ACTION: APPLY TRUTH

DAY TWO

INTERRUPT THE PATTERN BY APPLYING WHAT YOU KNOW

FOR THE SPIRIT GOD GAVE US DOES NOT MAKE US TIMID, BUT GIVES US POWER, LOVE AND *SELF-DISCIPLINE*. —2 TIMOTHY 1:7, AUTHOR'S EMPHASIS

In this verse the word translated "self-discipline" means using a sound mind, a settled and informed mind that is a gift from the Spirit. In this study, you have learned a lot about how your thoughts and fears are generated and the mechanics of how your brain works. Use what you know—use the power of your Holy Spirit-infused mind, filled with God's truth and the presence of the living Jesus. Let Him start making application of truth in the moments of your day.

Journal your experience. What did you learn? What did you observe?

_____

_____

_____

_____

_____

_____

THE WAY YOUR BRAIN WORKS IS PREDICTABLE AND ORDERLY, AND WE CAN COOPERATE WITH THE HOLY SPIRIT AS HE RENEWS OUR MINDS BY CHANGING OUR BRAINS. GOD WANTS TO IMPART TO US HIS OWN PEACE, AN INTERNAL STATE THAT EXTERNAL SITUATIONS CANNOT DISRUPT. HE TRANSFUSES YOU WITH HIS VERY OWN PEACE. NOTICE, NOT A PEACE LIKE HIS, BUT HIS PEACE. HOW CAN HE GIVE YOU HIS VERY OWN PEACE? BECAUSE HE LIVES IN YOU. RIGHT THIS MINUTE. IN THE MIDDLE OF THIS SITUATION. FULLY PRESENT IN ALL HIS POWER.

DAY THREE
TAKE ACTION: REACH OUT

INTERRUPT THE PATTERN BY REACHING OUT

For the Spirit God gave us does not make us timid, but gives us power, *LOVE* and self-discipline. —2 Timothy 1:7, author's emphasis

For Christ's love compels us, because we are convinced that one died for all, and therefore all died. And he died for all, that those who live should no longer live for themselves but for him who died for them and was raised again. —2 Corinthians 5:14–15

Grace, mercy and peace from God the Father and from Jesus Christ, the Father's Son, will be with us in truth and love. —2 John 1:3

Along with self-discipline, Paul lists love as the antithesis of fear. Love someone today in a way that is compelled by Christ's love. One way that fear gets the upper hand is when we get wrapped up in our own struggles and situations. Stop. Ask the Spirit to whom you should reach out in love today, and do it. Don't live for yourself, but for Him. Let Jesus express His love to someone today through you.

Journal your experience. What did you learn? What did you observe?

_____

_____

_____

_____

_____

_____

> YOU CAN INVITE HIM INTO YOUR
> EMOTIONAL MEMORY TO DO A DEEP
> WORK THAT HE ALONE CAN DO. HE
> CAN REMOVE THE TOXINS FROM THOSE
> MEMORIES AND LEAVE THEM POWER-
> LESS. YOU DON'T HAVE TO CONSCIOUSLY
> REMEMBER AN EVENT TO ASK THE
> SPIRIT, WHO SEARCHES THE DEEP AND
> HIDDEN THINGS, TO HEAL.

_____

_____

_____

_____

_____

_____

_____

_____

_____

TAKE ACTION: PRAY IN NEW WAYS
DAY FOUR

INTERRUPT THE PATTERN BY PRAYING IN NEW, CREATIVE WAYS

Be joyful in hope, patient in affliction, faithful in prayer.
—Romans 12:12

Rejoice always, pray continually, give thanks in all circumstances; for this is God's will for you in Christ Jesus.
—1 Thessalonians 5:16–18

Find some new ways to pray that will help you keep your mind on things above and not be caught up in fearful, worrying thoughts. In my book *Prayer Fatigue: 10 Ways to Revive Your Prayer Life*, I suggest some active ways to pray. Try some of these, or come up with your own.

1. Sing your prayers sometimes. No one is listening but God. Your prayer songs don't have to have either rhyme or rhythm. If this sounds silly to you right now, just try it. You'll see that it just engages you differently.

2. Sing hymns or praise choruses, or even listen to recorded praise music, and enter in with all your heart. As you are joining your heart with the words of the songs, specific people and situations you are praying about will come to mind, and the words will help you express your heart.

3. Walk through your house, and pray room by room sometimes.

4. Prayerwalk your neighborhood, letting the familiar sights trigger prayer.

5. Just do physical activity such as walking, jogging, treadmilling, or the like as you pray. Years ago, my mother used to walk a track for exercise, and that was her focused prayertime. Basically, she would pray for one person on her heart for one lap, then change topics at the next lap. She found that it kept her focused. All of us whose lives were the content of her prayers knew exactly what she meant when she said, "I gave you an extra lap today."

6. Write a note, an email, or a text of a prayer for a person on your heart. Do more than say, "I prayed for you." Consider writing out your prayer. With today's technology, you could even record a prayer in an audio file and text or email it.

Journal your experience. What did you learn? What did you observe?

_____

_____

_____

_____

_____

_____

_____

_____

_____
_____
_____
_____
_____
_____

> GOD IS NOT HAPHAZARD, BUT STRATEGIC.
> HE DOES NOT ALLOW ANYTHING TO COME INTO
> YOUR LIFE THAT IS NOT COMPATIBLE WITH AND
> NECESSARY TO HIS PLAN FOR YOUR GOOD, YOUR
> ULTIMATE HAPPINESS, YOUR BENEFIT. YOU
> CAN TRUST THAT WHEN PRAYER RELEASES THE
> POWER OF GOD FOR THE PURPOSES OF GOD INTO
> YOUR CIRCUMSTANCES, YOU WILL SEE HIS
> GOODNESS. THIS IS WHY YOUR HEART CAN REST
> IN HIM. WHEN YOU TURN TO HIM IN FAITH AND
> SURRENDER, HE WILL RESPOND WITH ALL HIS
> POWER AND ALL HIS PROVISION.

_____
_____
_____
_____
_____
_____
_____

TAKE ACTION: EXCHANGE LIES FOR TRUTH

(DAY FIVE)

INTERRUPT THE PATTERN BY DECLARING WHAT IS TRUE

MY TONGUE WILL PROCLAIM YOUR RIGHTEOUSNESS, YOUR PRAISES ALL DAY LONG. —PSALM 35:28

In our unredeemed state, Romans 1:25 says that sinful humanity (i.e., us) "exchanged the truth about God for a lie." Reverse that tactic. Every time the fearful lie starts wooing you, deliberately, in full sentences, declare the truth. If you are alone, do it out loud. If that is not an option, stop and write it down. Be as forceful and determined to get the truth into your mind as your enemy is to get the lie to stick.

Journal your experience. What did you learn? What did you observe?

_____

_____

_____

_____

_____

_____

_____

_____

WE CAN NAVIGATE LIFE, WITH
ALL ITS HARSH REALITIES AND
FRIGHTFUL POSSIBILITIES,
WITHOUT BEING HELD CAPTIVE TO
FEAR. FEAR DOES NOT HAVE TO RUN
THE SHOW. WE CAN LOOK LIFE'S
SITUATIONS IN THE EYE AND
STILL SAY, "WHOM SHALL I FEAR?"
WHEN WE KNOW GOD, AND
UNDERSTAND HIS HEART TOWARD
US, THERE IS NOTHING LEFT THAT
WE HAVE TO FEAR.

CONCLUSION

IN CONCLUSION, MEET SOME WOMEN, ALL FRIENDS OF MINE, WHO HAVE FACED AND OVERCOME FEAR. Let their stories encourage you.

CYNDY DUFFY

Bible study leader and encourager of women

My husband Tom had a 9 a.m. meeting at his headquarters office on the 99th floor of the North Tower of the World Trade Center on Tuesday morning of September 11, 2001. He never made that meeting, and he never came home. That was the day our country was attacked by terrorists, and nearly 3,000 people were killed.

As the fear of terror and unexpected loss enveloped my family and me, I sat in disbelief hanging between God's gripping hand and the abyss of spiraling darkness. I was surrounded by family, loving church friends, and neighbors. Everyone was in shock and confusion.

I asked Jesus to be my Lord and Savior at the age of 27 in 1976. I had a newborn son and loving husband, yet the emptiness in my heart yearned for more. When Jesus came into my life, that emptiness was filled, and I fell in love with the God of life and eternity. Through the ensuing years, Jesus became more real to me than even those around me. I was always hungering for more of Him and learning how faithful He was in every aspect of my life. When 9/11 happened I went to Jesus through God's Word because I knew that was the only place to find hope and freedom from the overwhelming fear surrounding me and the rest of the world around me. Although nothing made much sense in our world, God was the overarching, constant, and calm Presence that sustained me. By turning away from the horrors that raged and instead focusing on Jesus, His powerful, living words and presence calmed, comforted, and gave me protection and peace. Prayer, continual communing with Him, carried me through the hours, days, and weeks that followed. I always asked to pray with those who came to encourage me. God spoke to me through myriad Scriptures, and some that became bedrocks I held close to were Deuteronomy 33:27; Joshua 1:9; Psalm 23 and 139; Habakkuk 3:17–18; and Romans 8:28, 38–39. God gave me great peace in knowing Tom was with Him safe in heaven because of his personal faith in Jesus Christ (John 3:16).

God guided and protected me from the fear of harm to me and my family, the fear of being alone, and the fear of the future and assured me that just as He'd been with me all those past years, He would be with me now and in all the years ahead (Hebrews 13:5). Every time fear would sweep like a wave over my loved ones or me, I would go to the safest place I knew— Jesus and His faithful Word. I slept with my Bible so He was ever close through the night, and He spoke to me many times in the darkness, which was never dark to Him. Jesus soothed my weary soul. Jesus became my closest friend and He still is.

He has been faithful to me and to my family through a terrifying time and proven over and over He is greater and more powerful than any fear or loss.

DEBORAH LOVETT
Author and speaker

I had just sent an email to a friend asking for prayer because "I felt a little depressed." Little did I know the bottom was about to fall out. That's when "it" hit—the earth-shaking, horrific explosion. It was the end of my family's life as we knew it.

The explosion had shaken the entire house. Later, I heard that it shook the entire cul-de-sac next to our ranch. Now it shakes everyone who hears about it. Usually the people it shakes the most are the ones who need to be shaken. Comfortable people who think it can never happen to them. People like me.

Remember the days of drive-in movies? Everyone casually drinking sodas and eating popcorn, all eyes focused on the big screen as the latest drama unfolded in Technicolor. That's what it was like the evening my dreamworld died. Except in this scenario the drive-in theater was the horse pasture on our 22-acre property. People drove from miles around to park in our yard or on the road in front of our house, and then climbed through the slats in the horse fence to get a closer look. A couple hundred people had congregated before I could even grasp what was happening. All eyes were on the 3D, big screen destruction of my family's home. The five-year-old custom-designed home we built with dreams of living happily ever after was not looking like any fairy tale I had ever seen or heard.

Reality dawned the next morning, Sunday morning. After two hours of sleep, we went back home—except there was no home to go back to. Instead, we returned to the burial site of our former life. The morning light revealed a disaster of cataclysmic proportions, and we were in shock.

So if you ask me how to deal with fear of having nothing, fear of having your home burn to the ground, I would tell you that I learned many things. First, we will have trials and hardships, but the Lord will see us through. Secondly, don't worry about tomorrow for today is all you can handle. Thirdly, praise God and thank Him every day, it strengthens your faith, which is the opposite of fear. And now many years down the road, as I am writing this, I would say, less things means more family. We learned it is not the stuff that makes a home, but the people in it and, more importantly, we learned that dwelling in the house of the Lord is the only place worth living. So live happily, joyfully, and peacefully. God is faithful. Disappointments in life seem to be God's way of giving new reappointments. And in the end you can't take it with you. (Excerpt from *Arise Out of the Ashes*)

LEIGHANN MCCOY

Author and speaker

When I returned to the doctor after my second cancer diagnosis (colon cancer that was diagnosed as stage 1 recurred two years later in my liver, and I had surgery to remove the right lobe), he told my husband and me that while the surgery was somewhat successful, they were not able to get clear margins. That meant that according to lab reports, cancerous cells could still be in my liver. I knew I was facing six months of chemotherapy, but I didn't know that my liver surgeon was going to deliver a dire report. He proceeded to tell Tom and me that although chemo could stun cancer, it couldn't cure it, and that the likelihood that I'd have tumors return was 60 percent.

I'll never forget the way I felt as I received that news. I had just recovered from major surgery and was feeling pretty good about my recovery, but he took the wind right out of my sails. Tom and I were silent as we left his office and drove home. After a bit, I started talking about how my life on earth might be coming to an end, Tom asked me to stop talking about dying and just live until the time came. I knew it was hard for him, but just knowing that I couldn't talk freely about what was happening in me made me feel not only afraid but also alone.

Out of respect for him, we rode the rest of the way home in silence. I was feeling pretty sad, lonely, and, yes—if I admitted it freely—I was also afraid.

When we got home, I saw a box had been delivered just outside the garage door. I knew it was a box of books. When you publish a book, you receive a complimentary box of them as a "gift" to the author. It's always fun to see your work in its final form, so I eagerly tore into the box and found this book, *Oh God, Please Help Me with My Doubt*. It was a book I'd written some months earlier. I smiled because I knew that God saw how alone and afraid I felt. He reached right down from heaven and loved me through the delivery of my own book in His own time.

I've faced fear as I've walked out my faith. And every time I feel like I'm falling, God does something to let me know He's there, aware, willing and able. He either carries me through those fears, and I discover they are not so scary after all. Or He delivers me from them, and I find out they were never allowed to mess with me at all. God chooses which to do, and I am always better for it.

———————⊖———————

DEBBIE ALSDORF
Author and speaker

I remember the day, June 19, 2013. It was like any ordinary day with the exception of a routine mammogram. That timely medical test produced results that turned my world upside down and my heart inside out. When a doctor calls to tell you that you have cancer, fear immediately takes over. It's hard to think, it's surreal, and the future is scary. But in the middle of it all, I realized that God had prepared me for those test results. You see, for weeks I had been reading Psalm 103 every day. And, in that Psalm the words "Forget not all His benefits" seemed to pop out like a neon sign to my heart. Weeks later when gripped with the uncertainty of my situation, the words "forget not" flooded my mind. Yes, I had cancer. Yes, there would be treatment. Yes, this was a situation that could easily fill me with fear of the present and the unknown. But what was I to do? It was clear. I was to remember who He was and that He went with me into every treatment, machine, and procedure. I was to remind myself daily, sometimes hourly, that I was protected. Did I feel protected? Nope, after all I just found out I had cancer. But the truth remained, I was in His hands and protected. Fear has been a longtime battle in my life, and remembering Him in the midst of it has changed my life and soothed my fears over and over again.

———————————○———————————

FUELED BY FAITH

In these pages, I pray that you have found solid, structured answers. More than airy admonitions not to be afraid but concrete steps and explicit, sensible explanations to help you understand how to lean in to God's plan—the one He built into the structure of your mind and brain. For me, the more I understand tangible concepts, the more I cooperate with the processes God uses.

I celebrate with you that we don't have to live lives fueled by fear any longer. All the energy and time that worry and fear have consumed in our lives can be reallocated to joy and peace and worship and praise. Faith can run the show. I'd love to hear from you as you begin to experience fearless living. What changes?

> GOD IS A SAFE PLACE TO HIDE, READY TO HELP WHEN WE NEED HIM. WE STAND FEARLESS AT THE CLIFF-EDGE OF DOOM, COURAGEOUS IN SEA-STORM AND EARTHQUAKE, BEFORE THE RUSH AND ROAR OF OCEANS, THE TREMORS THAT SHIFT MOUNTAINS. —PSALM 46:1–3 *THE MESSAGE*

New Hope® Publishers is a division of WMU®, an international organization that challenges Christian believers to understand and be radically involved in God's mission. For more information about WMU, go to wmu.com. More information about New Hope books may be found at NewHopePublishers.com. New Hope books may be purchased at your local bookstore.

Use the QR reader on your smartphone to visit us online at NewHopePublishers.com.

If you've been blessed by this book, we would like to hear your story. The publisher and author welcome your comments and suggestions at newhopereader@wmu.org.

LIVE A PRAYING LIFE® SERIES

Whether for your own individual study or small group/church Bible study, the *Live a Praying Life®* series is timeless. National best-selling author Jennifer Kennedy Dean takes you back to the biblical basics of prayer, cleaning out myths about prayer to rev up a powerful, ongoing connection to God that can invigorate every aspect of a Christian's life.

LIVE A PRAYING LIFE®!
Jennifer Kennedy Dean
ISBN-13: 978-1-59669-436-1
$14.99

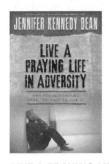

LIVE A PRAYING LIFE® IN ADVERSITY
Jennifer Kennedy Dean
ISBN-13: 978-1-59669-410-1
$11.99

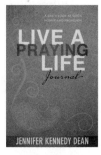

**LIVE A PRAYING LIFE®
JOURNAL**
Jennifer Kennedy Dean
ISBN-13: 978-1-59669-289-3
$14.99

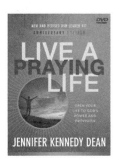

**LIVE A PRAYING LIFE®
DVD LEADER'S KIT
(Anniversary Edition)**
Jennifer Kennedy Dean
ISBN-13: 978-1-59669-290-9
$99.99

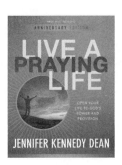

**LIVE A PRAYING LIFE®
WORKBOOK (Anniversary
Edition)**
Jennifer Kennedy Dean
ISBN-13: 978-1-59669-291-6
$14.99